GOLFER'S GUIDE

PORTUGAL

OVER 50 COURSES AND FACILITIES

MICHAEL GEDYE

NEW
HOLLAND

First published in the United Kingdom in 2001 by
New Holland Publishers (UK) Ltd
London • Cape Town • Sydney • Auckland

Garfield House	80 McKenzie Street	Unit 4, 14 Aquatic Drive	Unit 1A, 218 Lake Road
86 Edgware Road	Cape Town 8001	Frenchs Forest, NSW 2086	Northcote, Auckland
London, W2 2EA, UK	South Africa	Australia	New Zealand

1 3 5 7 9 10 8 6 4 2

ISBN 1 85974 403 6

Publishing manager: Jo Hemmings
Project manager: Elizabeth Mallard-Shaw
Design concept: Alan Marshall
Design: Alan Marshall and Chris Aldridge
Cartographer: William Smuts
Production controller: Joan Woodroffe
Indexer: Patricia Hymans

Reproduction by Pica Colour Separation Overseas (Pte) Ltd, Singapore
Printed and bound by Kyodo Printing Co (Singapore) Pte Ltd

Author's Acknowledgements
I am forever grateful to David Green, David Vansittart, Sir Henry Cotton, Visconde Pereira
Machado, Kenneth Clamp, Jorge Slewinski, Duarte Leal, Manuel Quintas and many others
for their past help and encouragement, allowing me to discover this most attractive country
and its people. Also to ICEP (London) for all their assistance in the preparation of this book.

Photographic Acknowledgements
All photographs taken by Michael Gedye except pages 15, 59, 88, 91 (ICEP), page 22
(Benamor Golf), page 68 (Oporto Golf Club), page 80 (Taylors), page 94 (Amarante Golf),
page 97 (Golfe Ponte de Lima) and page 98 (Geoffrey Farmer).

Front cover: *14th green, Old Course, Vilamoura*
Spine: *9th green, Palmares*
Back cover (anti-clockwise from top left): *16th hole, Royal Course, Vale do Lobo;
4th green, Palheiro, Madeira; Algarve fishing boats; 6th green, Penina; church in the Algarve*
Title page: *11th green, Ocean Course, Vale do Lobo*
Page 5: *11th green, Praia d'El Rey*

Contents

HOW TO USE THIS BOOK

Finding Your Course

The golf courses in this book are presented on a region-by-region basis. To find a specific course, you can look it up in the contents list or the index. Alternatively, if you are looking for a course in a particular location, consult the regional map at the beginning of each chapter then go to the appropriate number within the chapter for a full course description. Within each of the four regional chapters, the courses are arranged in a loosely geographical sequence which should assist you in planning an itinerary.

The 53 courses described are all that are open for play at the time of going to press, both in mainland Portugal and on its islands. Many further courses are either under construction or are planned for the future (see page 63). The most highly rated courses are described in depth, including a diagram of the course layout and a full card with hole distances and course length.

Golf Courses

Portuguese courses are measured in metres, and these measurements are given in each entry, together with an equivalent yardage. If you are accustomed to courses measured in yards, an easy approximate way to convert metres to yards is to add 10%. The overall lengths shown are the maximum length of the courses when played from the back tees. Individual hole distances mentioned in the descriptive text, unless otherwise stated, are also taken from the back tee on the scorecard.

The normal arrangement of tee markers is white for back (competition) tees, yellow for the normal, daily play tees and red for ladies. Occasionally, black or dark blue tee markers indicate an extreme back tee, which is used for professional events.

Club Facilities

All the courses included in this guide offer a range of facilities for golfers, and these are described in detail in the introduction to each course. Since the majority of Portuguese courses are primarily played by visitors, it is unusual to find separate changing or other facilities reserved for members. Although most clubs have shower facilities, not all provide towels and it is as well to take your own. All clubs have pull trolleys for hire, and also hire out good quality sets of clubs if you have not brought your own. Most now rent out golf carts as well, capable of carrying two players with their clubs. A few clubs even have caddies. An increasing number have roving snack vehicles touring the course.

Visitors' Restrictions

At the few clubs which are primarily for local members, there may be a restriction on visitors' tee times at weekends or if a course is staging a midweek competition. To avoid disappointment, it is advisable to telephone the course a day or two before your visit to reserve your starting time.

Most courses now require visiting players to have a handicap and many impose maximum limits for handicaps for both men and ladies, aimed at keeping play moving at a reasonable pace. Check the course entry in this guide and take a current handicap certificate with you. There will usually be a dress code, so avoid T-shirts and collarless shirts, jeans or beachwear. Clubs that require soft spikes are generally happy to change yours for you on request.

Key to Green Fees

For each course we have provided a rough guide to the green fee applicable, as follows:

E	=	*under 5,000 escudos*
EE	=	*5,000–8,999 escudos*
EEE	=	*9,000–12,999 escudos*
EEEE	=	*13,000–16,999 escudos*
EEEEE	=	*17,000 escudos and more*

These figures are based on the normal full midweek rate charged during the winter (peak golfing) season. Some clubs charge higher fees at weekends and some offer lower rates late in the afternoons. You will, however, probably be able to take advantage of a number of discount opportunitites, either through your travel operator, your hotel or by purchasing a golfing 'passport' booklet of reduced-fee vouchers.

Foreword

Portugal has become one of the most important golf destinations in the world, for along with its excellent courses of international standards it offers the golfer the added bonus of a warm and pleasant climate. I am sure that this book will help you to find the most interesting golf courses that our country has to offer.

On behalf of the Federation, I should like to welcome you to Portugal, and wish you an enjoyable stay.

Manuel Agrellos
Presidente, Federação Portuguesa de Golfe

Introduction

Golf in Portugal

For more than 30 years, holiday golfers have been visiting Portugal in increasing numbers. The country has become synonymous with the concept of resort golfing, especially during the winter. With its mild climate and low rainfall, it has proved ideal for holiday golf. However, any golfing visitor who fails to appreciate Portugal's many other attractions will have missed an enriching opportunity. As tourism has taken over as the mainstay of Portugal's economy, visitors have warmed to its courteous, friendly and hospitable people, and have been charmed by its culture and fine craftsmanship.

The country owes its unique character to a succession of past conquests and to its own pioneering and adventurous spirit. Celts, Phoenicians, Greeks, Carthaginians, Romans, Vizigoths and Moors all occupied Portugal, and left their mark in its architecture, language and cuisine.

Left: The 2nd at Tróia demands a heroic carry over sand to an angled, elevated green. Above: Parque da Floresta's par-3 11th is protected by palms and a lake.

An independent power from 1143, Portugal ranks as one of Europe's oldest nations. Throughout almost nine centuries of history, it has been influenced by the sea. Tucked away in the far south-west corner of Europe and bounded on two sides by 517 miles/832km of Atlantic coastline, it was in a unique position to explore the unknown and to develop international trade. Encouraged by Prince Henry the Navigator, 15th-century Portuguese explorers courageously ventured out to discover new worlds and bring their bounty back to Europe. In 1497, Vasco da Gama discovered the sea route to India; in 1500 Pedro Cabral reached Brazil. The Portuguese voyaged to Timor and China and in 1543 became the first Europeans to land in Japan. As the leading explorers of their time, they paved the way for the trade and wealth that made 16th-century Portugal one of the most powerful and wealthy countries in the western world, and left a rich and unique cultural heritage for visitors to enjoy today.

GOLF IN PORTUGAL

Despite its rapid growth, golf in Portugal is mainly a vacation resort activity. Even now, only 12,000 Portuguese play. The British lead the way as golfing visitors, making the Algarve their most popular overseas golf destination. Numbers from other countries, such as Germany, Sweden, Denmark and the Netherlands, are growing.

When to Play Golf

Golf is playable in Portugal all year round. There is no closed season because of snow or frost, and modern watering systems and drainage mean courses can be open every week of the year. However, most golfing holidays are taken during the winter season, between October and April, when hotels are less crowded and prices lower in the most popular areas. Most visiting golfers come from countries where golf is unattractive or even impossible in winter. In Portugal the winter is ideal for golf, with mild, sunny days and relatively little chance of rain.

Although golf is also perfectly playable in summer, the afternoon temperature, particularly in the south, is likely to be around 86°F/30°C. Most golfers choose to play in the early morning or late afternoon, when temperatures are more attractive.

GOLFING SCHOOLS

Although all clubs which employ a professional can offer individual lessons, there are a number which offer specific teaching packages, often for one week, through an academy. Examples include Parque da Floresta, the David Leadbetter academy at Carvoeiro, Pine Cliffs, the Butch Harmon Teaching Academy at Vilamoura, Pinheiros Altos and the Estoril-Sol International Academy. These schools are designed to attract both beginners and more experienced golfers who wish to improve their level of play through concentrated tuition.

Where to Play

Golf courses now exist throughout Portugal and its islands but the most popular areas for holiday golf, with the greatest choice of courses, are the Algarve coast and two regions close to Lisbon – the Costa Estoril and the Costa Azul. Between them, these three areas account for more than two-thirds of the golf in the country.

One of the attractions of playing golf in Portugal, however, apart from the appeal of playing sun-drenched green fairways in warm weather, is the wide diversity of location and terrain you can experience, combined with the confidence of knowing that, in most cases, the courses have been built by modern construction methods and are well irrigated and drained, with grasses suited to the climate. You can play on seaside links with grassy dunes or tackle elegant parkland layouts lined with majestic trees. There is mountain golf with spectacular views and island courses carved out of volcanic slopes. You can tackle tough championship examinations that have tested the top professionals or relax with less demanding but equally interesting designs in seductive settings. In a wide variety of locations, there is golf for all, whatever their ability or level of interest.

Golf Etiquette and Restrictions

All golf clubs in Portugal welcome visiting players but generally require some evidence of proficiency, such as a handicap certificate from the home club, to protect the interests of other players and assist the speed of play. A current handicap certificate will also be useful if you wish to enter a competition. Clubs may well specify maximum handicaps.

The use of soft spikes is often stipulated, and many clubs operate a dress code. This, in essence, discourages clothing more suited to the beach than a golf course and definitely precludes the wearing of jeans.

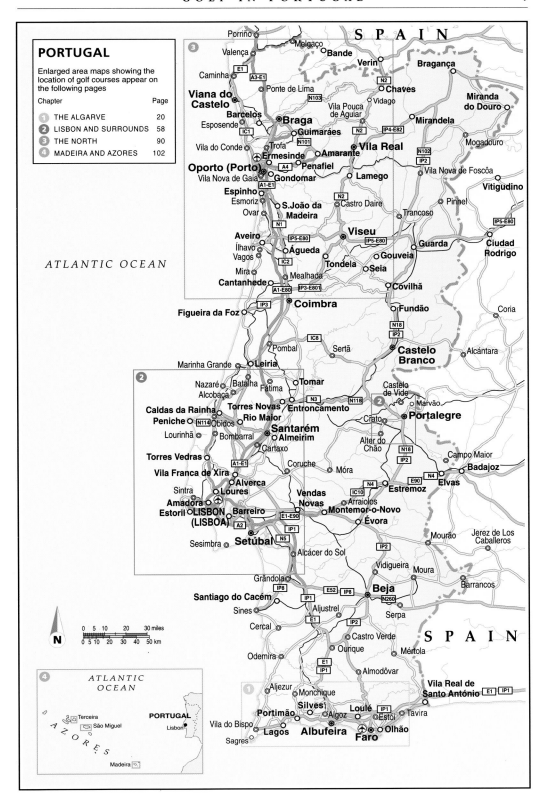

PORTUGAL

Enlarged area maps showing the
location of golf courses appear on
the following pages

Normal aspects of golfing etiquette are encouraged, particularly when courses are busy. These will include avoiding slow play, not sharing clubs, raking bunkers, replacing divots and observing club restrictions in respect of trolleys or golf carts.

Specialist Tour Operators

During the past 30 years, the market for holiday golf has grown sufficiently to support a number of specialist tour operators. These companies can put together attractive packages to popular golfing destinations, to include return flight, hotel, breakfast, self-drive car or transfer and, generally, a number of rounds at specified courses or specially discounted green fees. In some cases, pre-booked tee times are also included in the package. These complete golfing packages are invariably a cheaper option than making your own arrangements. The tour operators can offer special arrangements for groups and tailor-made packages; they also organize competition weeks for clients or arrange packages around existing local competitions, such as the Estoril International Golf Week or the Vale de Lobo Amateur Week.

Travel Tips for the Golfer

Comprehensive travel insurance is advisable, and, if you are taking your golf clubs with you, ensure that the policy will cover them in the event of their loss. It is a good idea to pack your golf bag within an outer, lockable cover. This ensures the safe transit of small items, such as golf balls, and reduces wear and possible damage to the golf bag and clubs. There is no need to take your trolley as every club has them for rent. Although most clubs have well-stocked pro shops, some golfing items can be expensive in Portugal. It is wise, therefore, to take gloves and an adequate supply of balls.

Whatever time of year you travel, the sun will be strong. Take a suitable factor sun-protection cream and lip balm, but also accept that the sun does not shine all the time. Pack your golf umbrella and waterproofs, just in case. You may also need a sweater during the winter season, especially early or late in the day. Although you may need a phrase book in shops or small restaurants, all resort golf clubs have bilingual staff, with English a common language. Fortunately, the terminology of golf is universal anyway.

Three useful publications which are circulated free to Portuguese golf clubs and some hotels are the bimonthly *Sun Golf*, which covers golfing news and features in both Portugal and Spain, and, in the Algarve, the quarterly *Algarve Golf & Leisure* and the monthly *Algarve Golf Guide*.

TOUR OPERATORS

Leading specialist tour operators to Portugal include the following, all based in Britain:

3D Golf (01292 263 331)
Algarve Golf Agency (01204 595 222)
Algarve Select (01625 588 430)
Amersham Travel (01494 738 277)
Apollo Travel Group (01709 301 333)
Bill Goff Golf Tours (0191 427 5003)
British Airways Holidays (01293 722 727)
Caravela Tours (020 7630 5148)
Club Travel 2000 (0161 445 2916)
Exclusive Golf Tours (020 8679 6571)
Golf and Leisure Breaks (01491 576 861)
Gulliver's Sports Travel (01684 293 175)
KB Golf (01254 235 608)
Leisure Link Golf Holidays International (01277 228 980)
Leisure Pursuits Group (01256 471 016)
Longmere Golf (020 8655 2075)
Longshot Golf Holidays (01730 268 621)
Lotus Supertravel (020 7962 9494)
Premier Iberian Golf Holidays (01327 350 394)
Select World Golf (01202 701 881)
Serenity Golf (01794 517 000)

End of the day on the 197yd/180m 15th hole at Penha Longa (Atlantico), a beautiful par-3 set on higher ground, offering outstanding views over the course.

TRAVELLING TO AND IN PORTUGAL

Entry Requirements

Visitors from within the EU need only produce their passport or identity card and can stay for up to 90 days. Nationals of other countries may need a visa and the period of stay may differ.

Customs

Visitors may bring in duty-free up to 200 cigarettes or 100 small cigars or 50 large cigars or 250gm tobacco; 1 litre spirits or 2 litres liqueurs; 2 litres table wine plus 50gm perfume or 250ml toilet water. Visitors from an EU member state can theoretically bring in unlimited duty-paid amounts of these items for personal use, although as both alcohol and tobacco are relatively cheap in Portugal, there seems little point. There is no limit on the import of money for travel expenses but customs should be informed if the total value exceeds 2.5 million escudos.

Health Requirements

All visitors should have travel insurance covering emergency medical care and, if necessary, repatriation. Non-resident EU citizens should have forms E111 and E112 in case they require access to health services during their stay. Visitors coming from an affected area will need a certificate of vaccination against yellow fever.

Getting There

TAP Air Portugal (Lisbon tel: 21 841 6990), the country's national carrier with direct international flights into Lisbon, Oporto, Faro and Funchal (Madeira), has an excellent reputation for quality service and being 'golfer friendly'.

Baggage allowance is 44lb/20kg Economy Class and 66lb/30kg Navigator Class. Each passenger leaving and returning to the UK may take one golf bag free in addition to this allowance. From other countries, a golf bag is weighed with other baggage, but any excess charge on it is based on 33lb/15kg being rated as 13lb/6kg. The airline organizes an annual 72-hole strokeplay golf tournament in the Algarve

ROAD SIGNS

Although Portugal uses international road signs,
here are a few words it's useful to recognize.

Abrande • Slow down
Atenção • Attention
Cuidado • Caution
Curva perigosa • Dangerous bend
Dê prioridade • Give way
Desvio • Diversion
Espere • Wait
Estacionamento proibido • No parking
Obras na estrada • Road works
Parque de estacionamento • Car park
Passagem proibida • No entry
Perigo • Danger

each November, with competitors coming from many countries.

If you are planning an extended stay, driving may be an option. From the UK, car ferries sail over 24 hours to Santander and Bilbao in northern Spain, but these ferry services are either less frequent or suspended in the winter season.

Getting Around
By air
TAP Air Portugal operates daily flights from Lisbon to Oporto and Faro, and connects with Horta, Terceira and Ponta Delgada in the Azores and Funchal and Porto Santo in Madeira. Portugalia (midweek 21 842 5559/60/61/62; weekends 21 385 5562) also has regular domestic flights between Lisbon, Oporto and Faro as well as a number of European cities. SATA-Air Açores (296 282 311) connects within the various Azores islands and to Lisbon.

By road
Car hire Car rental is available at all main airports and in major towns. Expect to find the leading international names as well as local firms. Most golf package holidays include a car but otherwise it pays to book

ahead, especially in peak seasons, not only to ensure the car you want but often a cheaper deal as well. You will need to have held your current driving licence for over a year, be over 21 and produce a passport or identity card. The green card is obligatory; it is as well to have full personal and collision damage insurance in addition to third party.

Rules of the road The Portugese drive on the right, at least most of the time. Driving a car here requires extreme vigilance and an acceptance that your fellow motorists are quite likely to do the unexpected. Normally charming and placid, put a Portuguese (usually male) behind the wheel of a car and he is transformed into a motoring monster. Impatience and recklessness become the norm, such as overtaking on blind bends and just before the brow of a hill. This no doubt accounts for the fact that the country has a fatality rate of 35 per 100,000 population compared to 7 per 100,000 in the UK. The worst stretch of road is the EN125, which runs the length of the Algarve and is particularly hazardous. Portuguese drivers seem unable to foresee the possible consequences of any rash motoring act. You have been warned. Speed limits are 50kph (30mph) in built-up areas, 90kph (55mph) on normal roads, 100kph (62mph) on national roads (with N or EN prefix) and 120kph (75mph) on motorways.

Keep the tank full, especially in rural areas at weekends, and look out for farm vehicles and animals on minor roads. Always have your passport with you and be aware that any driver found with more than 0.5gm/litre of blood alcohol can be punished severely with a heavy fine or imprisonment. Traffic violations by non-residents can be dealt with by on-the-spot fines. Seatbelt use is compulsory front and rear and infringement carries a heavy fine.

Taxis There are ranks in major towns and also radio taxis. Tariffs are set for within and without city limits, with a higher rate applying between 22:00 and 06:00 on weekdays and for weekends and national holidays. Short journeys are charged by meter; for a longer distance, you may negotiate a charge in advance. An additional charge can be made for accompanied luggage and a radio taxi phone call. All toll payments are the responsibility of the customer. Tips are voluntary and about 10%. The taxi charge can include four passengers.

Buses The location of most golf clubs will generally prove unsuitable for bus travel, which in rural areas acts as a link between towns and villages. However, they may prove attractive in large cities. Timetables are posted at bus stops and bus stations.

Colourful fishing boats on the beach at Armação de Pêra, in the central Algarve, in daily use to ensure a fresh catch for the many nearby restaurants.

By rail

A network of express trains serves the entire mainland, with intercity links between Lisbon and both Oporto and Faro, as well as international rail links. Lisbon has an extensive underground system. There is a regular rail service between Cascais/Estoril and Lisbon.

ACCOMMODATION

Most golf tour operator packages and, indeed, most golfing holidays, are based on hotel accommodation, often close to the anticipated golf course or courses. Hotels are graded with from 1 to 5 stars and priced accordingly. In many cases, guests can enjoy preferential green fee rates negotiated by the hotel with local golf courses.

An alternative is an *estalagem*, which is an inn of quality with 4 or 5 stars offering rather less formal accommodation than a hotel. An a*lbergaria* is a 4-star inn similar to an *estalagem*.

'Aparthotels' offer high quality self-catering accommodation. These will usually have a restaurant and possibly other facilities such as a swimming pool and shops. Many golf developments include individual apartments and villas which will accommodate from two to possibly eight people. There are also *pensão* (pensions) and *residencial* (bed and breakfast only), which are basic boarding houses ranging from 2 to 4 stars.

Two national initiatives which have proved popular are *pousadas* and *turismo de habitação*. The former, now a national chain of more than 40 properties, comprise sympathetic conversions of historic castles, monasteries and other classified national monuments or stately buildings in areas of outstanding natural beauty. They are graded into categories and offer high-quality service and accommodation with an accent on regional cuisine, making a stay in one a unique cultural experience. The programme of *turismo de habitação* allows visitors to stay in family-run mansions and manor houses of recognized historic and architectural beauty. This not only affords closer contact with the traditions and customs of a region but also provides an interesting form of accommodation, particularly in rural areas where few hotels are available.

FOOD AND DRINK

One of the genuine delights of foreign travel is the opportunity to discover new tastes, new sensations, the chance to experience different ways of life. Visitors to Portugal should be sure to explore a cuisine that is both unique and full of interest, quite unlike that of its near neighbour Spain, and rich in the influence of history.

Bordered on two sides by the Atlantic, the geographical position of the country gave it strategic and commercial importance down the centuries linked to its inevitable growth as a nation of seafarers. Isolated from mainland Europe, its varied menu has benefited from the import of precious spices, rice and tea from the Far East; peanuts, coffee, broad beans and fruits from Africa; and pineapple, peppers, tomatoes and potatoes from the New World. The national staple, salt cod (see page 91), grew out of the need to preserve fish that had been caught on long sea voyages. The diversity of natural produce has played its part - succulent seafood on the coasts, freshwater fish inland, dairy produce, pork and green vegetables virtually everywhere. A flair for unusual combinations has created such culinary triumphs as salt cod with eggs and olives, clams with spicy sausage and fresh trout with ham.

Look for soups such as *caldo verde* (cabbage, potato and garlic sausage) or *acorda de mariscos* (a 'dry' soup of country bread, shrimp, eggs and onion flavoured with garlic, chillis, white wine and coriander). The harvest of the sea is rich in variety. Apart from cod, try *sardinhas grelhadas* (grilled sardines), *bife de atum* (tuna steak), *linguado* (sole), *espadarte fumado* (smoked swordfish), *robalo* (sea bass), *sapateira* (crab) and *lagosta* (lobster). Other popular dishes include *arroz de marisco* (seafood rice), *porco a Alentejana* (pork loin steamed with clams) and *espetada* (skewers of beef with garlic and bay leaves). There are fine traditional sweetmeats based on sugar and egg yolks, delicious *pasteis de nata* (light custard tarts with cinnamon) and many cheeses (*queijo*) made from both cows' and goats' milk.

Some wines are said 'not to travel well', and in the case of Portugal, it is certainly true. In spite of the large amount of wine produced (Portugal is sixth in the world league of wine-producing countries), the relative isolation and poverty of the people has ensured such enthusiasm for their own

A traditional cataplana *filled with steamed clams, prawns and sliced, smoked sausage – a culinary speciality.*

product that they are second in global wine consumption, drinking over three-quarters of their annual output.

Most of the Portuguese wine drunk abroad, such as Mateus and Lancers rosé, would not be touched by the locals. They have a superb range of wines, both red and white, which can be an eye-opener for the unprepared visitor and is a fitting complement to the rich and varied cuisine.

From the far north comes *vinho verde*, both red and white, light, crisp and very popular. From the steeply terraced vinyards along the Douro River, come not only fine red and white table wines but also the fortified wine which is the country's best-known product – port. The central region produces some of the best red wines – Dão, Bairrada, Estramadura and Ribatejo. From west of Lisbon come three notable, if small labels: Colares, Bucelas and Carcavelos. Around the Sado estuary and the attractive Arrabida peninsula, excellent wines from Palmela and Azeitão are available, as well as

the renowned Moscatel of Setubal. A number of interesting wines are now emerging from the Alentejo, especially reds, and are well worth looking for. Finally, there are the uniquely produced fortified wines from the island of Madeira.

TRAVEL FACTS AND TIPS

Currency

The unit of currency is the escudo. Each unit (1$00) is divided into 100 centavos. Escudos are shown to the left of a $ sign and centavos to the right, and 1,000$00 is called a *conto*. Bank notes have face values of 10,000$00, 5,000$00, 2,000$00, 1,000$00 and 500$00. Coins are 200$00, 100$00, 50$00, 20$00, 10$00, 5$00, 2$50 and $50.

Portugal has adopted the Euro, now in use for all payments made through the banking system. Until 31 December 2001, payments in notes and coins will be made in escudos and both currencies will be shown on bills.

VAT at 17% is included in bills. Visitors from outside the EU whose stay is less than 180 days are exempt and can be reimbursed for purchases at airports on departure – allow extra time in case of delays.

Travellers Cheques and Credit Cards

Travellers cheques can be exchanged at the desk marked '*Câmbios*' in a bank and in most hotels. You will need your passport.

The most widely accepted credit cards are Visa, American Express, EC-Eurocheque, Eurocard, Mastercard and Diners Club. There is a national network of automatic cash machines (look for the sign 'MB') available 24 hours a day. The maximum daily withdrawal is 40,000$00.

Tipping

A service charge is automatically added to hotel and restaurant bills but a tip of 5–10% is usually added for good service.

Business Hours

Normal opening hours for shops are 9:00–13:00 and 15:00–19:00 Monday to Friday. From January to November, shops close at 13:00 on Saturday, but in December they are also open 15:00–19:00. Some shopping centres open longer, generally 10:00–24:00. Banking hours are 08:30–15:30 Monday to Friday.

What to Wear

The country has a mild climate, with relatively little rainfall except in the northern regions and the islands in winter. Average temperatures are fairly consistent, although it is generally cooler in the north and can be hot in summer in the south.

Take lightweight clothing in the summer season, always remembering that normal standards of decorum should apply when visiting golf clubs. From autumn through spring, you may need some warmer clothes and the odd sweater, especially in early mornings and evenings. Be prepared for the occasional shower, especially in winter.

The Portuguese are fairly conservative in dress, favouring sombre colours. On formal golfing occasions, such as tournament prizegivings or cocktail parties, you will find the organizers wearing jacket and tie and it would be as well to pack some suitable clothes for these.

Etiquette

Portuguese people are extremely courteous and polite. It is normal for them to accompany such greetings as '*Bom dia*' with a handshake or kisses. Apart from such social niceties, they are basically relaxed and informal, tolerant of the ways of others and with much natural charm. Noisy, inconsiderate behaviour should be avoided, however; also excessive drinking.

Communications

Post offices are open 09:00–18:00 Monday to Friday. Central post offices and those at airports are open on Saturdays. Stamps are sold at post offices, street kiosks and at all locations marked with a red horse or a white circle on a green background.

Telephone kiosks are marked 'Portugal Telecom'. Payment can be by coins, Credifone or Telecom Card (sold in Telecom Portugal shops, post offices, kiosks and tobacconists) and some compatible credit and debit cards.

Time Difference

Mainland Portugal and Madeira are on GMT in winter. From 01:00 on the last Sunday in March until 02:00 on the last Sunday in October, time is put forward one hour. The Azores are one hour behind mainland Portugal.

PUBLIC HOLIDAYS AND FESTIVALS

On the days listed below, almost everything is closed and public transport much reduced. Local holidays may also affect public opening times.

New Year's Day • 1 January
Carnival • variable
Good Friday • variable
Liberty Day • 25 April
Labour Day • 1 May
Corpus Christi • variable
Portugal Day • 10 June
St Anthony's Day ★ • 13 June
St John's Day ★★ • 24 June
The Assumption of Our Lady • 15 August
Founding of the Republic • 5 October
All Saints Day • 1 November
Restoration of Independence • 1 December
Immaculate Conception • 8 December
Christmas Day • 25 December

★ Bank holiday only in Lisbon
★★ Bank holiday only in Oporto

GETTING BY IN PORTUGUESE

Numbers

1 • *um*   8 • *oito*
2 • *dois*   9 • *nove*
3 • *trés*   10 • *dez*
4 • *quatro* 11 • *onze*
5 • *cinco* 12 • *doze*
6 • *seis*   20 • *vinte*
7 • *sete*   21 • *vinte e um*

Days of the Week

Sunday • *domingo*
Monday • *segunda-feira*
Tuesday • *terça-feira*
Wednesday • *quarta-feira*
Thursday • *quinta-feira*
Friday • *sexta-feira*
Saturday • *sábado*

Colours

white • *branco*
black • *preto*
red • *encarnado*
blue • *azul*
green • *verde*

brown • *castanho*
yellow • *ararelo*
pink • *cor de rosa*
grey • *cinzento*
dark • *escuro*
light • *claro*

Greetings and Remarks

hello • *olá*
good morning • *bom dia*
good afternoon/evening • *boa tarde*
good night • *boa noite*
goodbye • *adeus*
please • *por favor*
thank you • *obrigado*
(as a woman) • *obrigada*
yes • *sim*
no • *não*

Phrases

Please help me • *Ajude-me por favor*
Where is...? • *Onde é...?*

Where is the lavatory? • *Onde ficam os lavabos?*
What is the address? • *Qual o endereco?*
What is the phone number? • *Qual o numero de telefone?*
How much is it? • *Quanto custa?*
Do you speak English? • *Fala ingles?*
I am looking for... • *Estou procurando...*
I want to cash this traveller's cheque • *Quero trocar esta cheque de viajante*

Useful Words

entrance • *entrada*
exit • *saida*
no smoking • *proibido fumar*
open • *abre*
close • *fecha*
guide book • *um roteiro*
map • *um mapa*
petrol station • *bomba de gasolina*

Electricity

Voltage is 220/380 volts at 50 Hertz; sockets take standard European two-pin plugs.

Weights and Measures

Portugal has adopted the metric system.

Health Services

For primary medical care, go to the nearest health centre (*centro de saúde*). There is one in every town and major cities have many. Some have permanent emergency servicès called SAP/CATUS. Hospital emergency services (*servicos de urgencia dos hospitais*) should be used only in very serious situations such as severe trauma, poisoning, burns, heart attacks, strokes or breathing difficulties. There are also private clinics.

For access to health services, EU citizens not resident in Portugal should have their passport or identity card plus forms EE111 and E112. Within the public services, the patient has to pay a modest fee before receiving medical assistance.

Chemists (*farmacia*) can be identified by a green cross, illuminated at night if the chemist is on duty, When closed, they will display a notice indicating the nearest duty chemist, open 24 hours a day. Alternatively, you can dial 118 for the same information.

Emergencies

In case of emergency, dial 112 (no payment required) and ask for *policia* (police), *bombeiros* (fire services) or *ambulância* (ambulance). The emergency services operator may speak only Portuguese, so try to have a local person assist you.

Chapter 1

The Algarve

Tucked away along Portugal's southern coastline, the Algarve has always seemed remote and dissimilar to the country further north. Even its name, coming from the Arabic *el gharb*, means 'the land beyond'. For it was the Moors from Africa who left the most indelible mark on the region, its crafts and culture, giving it a character all its own. Not long ago, before the inexorable tide of tourism created a whole new economy, life moved at a gentle pace, relaxed and undisturbed for centuries, based on the staples of fishing and agriculture. For the visitor, the essential charm and beauty of the region remains and will reward research away from tourist locations.

Few coastal regions can claim a more attractive climate: hot and sunny in summer but tempered by cooling Atlantic breezes; mild and sunny in winter with

Left: Cultural influences are evident in the architecture of the Algarve's many ornate village churches. Above: Typical rugged cliffs along the coast of the western Algarve.

only occasional showers. The advent of charter flights and inexpensive package holidays in the late 1950s opened up the coast as a reliable, reachable summer alternative for northern Europeans; the introduction of resort golf, at Penina in 1966, provided the catalyst for hotels to remain open all year and attract a different, out-of-season market – golfers. Such was its success that the region can now boast 19 resort golfing locations with a total 369 holes – and more to come.

The coastal scenery of the Algarve ranges from gently idyllic to wildly dramatic. Craggy rock outcrops and red weathered sandstone cliffs loom over sparkling sun-drenched beaches, washed by the clear Atlantic tides. At the western end, at Sagres, the most south-westerly point in Europe, Prince Henry the Navigator (1394–1460) established a school of scientific navigation, which launched the profusion of Portuguese explorers whose skills opened up the unknown world and helped make

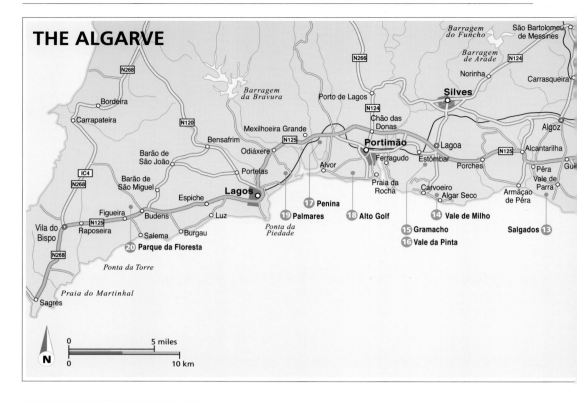

THE ALGARVE

Barragem do Funcho · São Bartolomeu de Messines · N266 · Barragem de Arade · N124 · Norinha · Carrasqueira · N268 · Barragem da Bravura · Porto de Lagos · Silves · Algoz · Bordeira · Carrapateira · N120 · Chão das Donas · N124 · Mexilhoeira Grande · Portimão · Lagoa · N125 · Alcantarilha · Bensafrim · N125 · Odiáxere · Ferragudo · Estômbar · Porches · Gu · Barão de São João · Alvor · Pêra · Vale de Parra · Portelas · Praia da Rocha · Carvoeiro · IC4 · N268 · Barão de São Miguel · Espiche · **Lagos** · Algar Seco · Armação de Pêra · Figueira · Budens · Luz · 🅱 **Penina** · Carvoeiro · Vila do Bispo · N125 · Raposeira · Salema · Burgau · Ponta da Piedade · 🅳 **Palmares** · 🅸 **Alto Golf** · 🅵 **Gramacho** · Salgados 🅳 · N268 · 🄴 **Parque da Floresta** · 🅶 **Vale da Pinta** · 🅴 **Vale de Milho** · Ponta da Torre · Praia do Martinhal · Sagres

0 ———— 5 miles
0 ———— 10 km
N

OUT OF AFRICA

Isolated from the rest of Portugal by mountains, the Algarve coast has been attracting merchant explorers and colonists since 1000 BC. Most significant has been the influence of the Moors from North Africa, who for 500 years ruled and developed the Algarve. Their legacy remains not only in local crops such as oranges, lemons, almonds and rice, but in the distinctive local architecture and design. Low, flat-roofed houses, pastel-washed in contrasting colours, proudly boast unique decorative chimneys – their fretted white shapes reflecting Arab influence – and low latticed walls. Look also for the many decorative ceramic designs, mainly blue and white, which decorate wall tiles and hand-painted pottery produced in the region. Other traces of the North African influence can be found in the local cuisine, where herbs and spices feature; also the use of the *cataplana* for steaming.

Portugal the world's wealthiest nation at the turn of the 16th century. Trading has been replaced by tourism as the mainstay of the Portuguese economy, with the Algarve the magnet, particularly for northern European golfers in winter.

Away from the fairways, there is much to fascinate and to be explored: small, often isolated villages, their winding cobbled streets leading to ancient fortifications and churches like white sculpted confections. The charm and innate courtesy of the locals is infectious; the culture is absorbing. Regular festivals and religious holidays provide ample excuses for processions, vibrant music, singing and colourful folk dancing. Local markets offer fine examples of wood and leather crafts, needlework and ceramics.

For the gourmet, there is a rich harvest from the sea, complemented by fresh

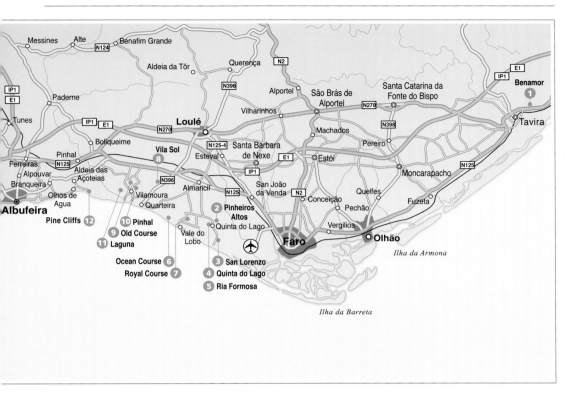

produce grown inland. One enduring memory has to be the scent of freshly grilled sardines, supplemented by swordfish steaks and a full range of succulent seafood. Notable dishes include *amêijoas na cataplana* (clams steamed with sausage, ham, garlic and onions), *leitão assado* (roast suckling pig), *arroz de marisco* (seafood rice) and *bacalhau a brás* (cod, potatoes and scrambled egg). Cakes and sweet puddings are based on almonds, honey, figs and eggs; there is also a wealth of fresh fruit to enjoy.

The Algarve is not noted for its wines, which tend to be alcoholic and undistinguished. Just north, however, in the Alentejo, great potential is at last being realized under such labels as Quinta do Carmo and Esporão. For a local liqueur, try *amêndoa amarga*, a distillation of almonds or, for the truly courageous, the local firewater, *medronho*.

Below: Strong North African influence remains in the clean lines, flat roofs and unique filigree chimneys of Algarve houses.

 ## *Benamor*

Quinta da Benamor Golf, 8800-067 Conceição, Tavira, Algarve
TEL: *(281) 320880* **FAX:** *(281) 320888*
LOCATION: *22 miles/35km east of Faro on EN125*
COURSE: *18 holes, 5951yd/5440m, par 71, SSS 71*
TYPE OF COURSE: *Rolling land with established trees*
DESIGNER: *From a design concept by Sir Henry Cotton (2000)*
GREEN FEES: *EE*
FACILITIES: *Pro shop, cart, trolley and equipment hire, tuition, club-fitting, driving range with additional teaching location and target greens, putting green and putting course, changing facilities, bar and restaurant in clubhouse*
VISITORS: *Handicap certificate required; soft spikes only*

First star in the east, Benamor heralds a new expansion in the Algarve's golfing history. It opens up the prospect of a series of golfing developments along the hitherto undisturbed coastal stretch east of Faro, linking with the Spanish border and courses just beyond.

In 1986, the late Sir Henry Cotton visited the untouched, undulating site at Benamor, just east of the historic fishing village of Tavira, and fell in love with the location, not least the quaint white church (built in 1750) which sits next to the new timber clubhouse. He produced a design concept which,

The course flows around an attractive central clubhouse right by the beautiful old 18th-century church, with superb views of wooded mountain slopes beyond.

incorporating various amendments through the intervening years, has produced an interesting golf course in an outstanding setting. The Cotton legend lives on.

With views to distant hills and protected wildlife habitats flanking the sea, this rolling course will prove an interesting test, despite its limited length. Studded with olive, cork, carob and almond trees, the Bermuda-grass fairways flow over gentle slopes to attractive Penncross bent greens. Good use is made of strategic sand and lakes (water is in play on eight holes), and the natural contours of the land, to create entertaining golf. This is summed up in the par 5, 4, 3, 5 finish, with the final hole a testing 559yd/511m dogleg finishing in front of the clubhouse.

A novel feature is the putting course, sure to be the venue of many post-round drinks matches, which is sited just below the clubhouse terrace *en route* to the practice ground. Opened in spring 2000, future plans include a hotel and villa development.

2 Pinheiros Altos

Pinheiros Altos Campo de Golfe, Apartado 2168, Quinta do Lago, 8135 Almancil, Algarve
TEL: *(289) 359910* **FAX:** *(289) 394392*
LOCATION: *12 miles/20 km west of Faro on Quinta do Lago estate via Almancil on EN125*
COURSE: *18 holes, 6765yd/6186m, par 72, SSS 72*
TYPE OF COURSE: *Part running over hilly, pine-forested terrain; part across low-lying marshland*
DESIGNER: *Ronald Fream, with later amendments to back nine by Peter McEvoy and Howard Swann (1992)*
GREEN FEES: *EEEE*
FACILITIES: *Pro shop, cart, trolley and equipment hire, multilingual tuition in golf academy, putting and chipping greens, driving range, roving on-course snack buggy, changing facilities, bar and restaurant in clubhouse*
VISITORS: *Valid handicap certificate: men 28, ladies 45; dress code; soft spikes only*

Opened in 1992 and one of three courses in the Algarve created by the noted Californian architect Ronald Fream, this is a golf course of two quite distinct halves. The front nine runs over and along a sandy hillside graced with a rich covering of umbrella pines. Steep slopes, well-bunkered, elevated greens and some heroic carries, most notably at the 174yd/159m par-3 5th across a deep wooded chasm between tee and green, provide an exhilarating start to the round.

The second nine, in complete contrast, flows out over level marshland on the borders of the environmentally protected Ria Formosa nature reserve, offering the prospect of a variety of birdies, if only of the feathered kind. Bereft of trees, these holes more than compensate with stretches of strategic water, which come into play on every hole but one.

Visitors will remember the par-3 17th, with its island green, set invitingly within a lake, a mere 136yd/124m away. With sloping edges and one deep, magnetic sand trap, it requires good club selection in any breeze and a positive shot. Another fine hole is the shortish 360yd/329m 4th, where out-of-bounds and a bunker well-sited on the right-hand dogleg demand accuracy, as does the approach to a downhill shelf of green protected by trees on the left.

There is a comprehensive golf academy, much favoured by wintering tournament pros, and a superb clubhouse, whose terraces afford views over the course. Future plans include a further nine holes and a health spa.

The second shot to the par-4 9th (see page 54) requires careful placement to avoid the hazards.

3 San Lorenzo

San Lorenzo Golf Club, Quinta do Lago, 8135 Almancil,
Algarve
TEL: *(289) 396522* FAX: *(289) 396908*
LOCATION: *12 miles/20km west of Faro on Quinta do
Lago estate via Almancil on EN125*
COURSE: *18 holes, 6822yd/6238m, par 72, SSS 73*
TYPE OF COURSE: *Undulating sandy land with a wealth
of pine, bordering a seaside lagoon*
DESIGNER: *Joseph Lee; built by Rocky Roquemore (1988)*
GREEN FEES: *Meridien Hotel guests EE; Visitors EEEEE*
FACILITIES: *Pro shop, cart, trolley and equipment hire,
tuition, putting green, driving range, changing facilities,
on-course snack buggy, bar and restaurant in clubhouse*
VISITORS: *Handicap certificate required; maximum: men
28, ladies 36; strict dress code; soft spikes only*

SAN LORENZO

HOLE	YD	M	PAR	HOLE	YD	M	PAR
1	540	494	5	10	567	519	5
2	177	162	3	11	383	350	4
3	366	334	4	12	432	395	4
4	371	339	4	13	393	359	4
5	141	129	3	14	172	157	3
6	422	386	4	15	517	473	5
7	377	345	4	16	208	190	3
8	574	525	5	17	376	344	4
9	400	366	4	18	406	371	4
OUT	3368	3080	36	IN	3454	3158	36

6822 YD • 6238M • PAR 72

Life at the top is never easy and a high ranking is inevitably hard to live up to. San Lorenzo, open since 1988, has consistently rated highly in the annual *Golf World* rankings, having featured as high as second best in Europe and currently settled at number 5. Judgements by a panel are notoriously subjective and never more so than with golf, but in the case of this underplayed

star they are close to the mark. The course was designed by an American, Joe Lee, and built by another, Rocky Roquemore. Few golf architects are presented with such an attractive setting on which to lay out a resort golf course. The result combines length, a fair measure of strategic difficulty and highly enjoyable, scenic golf. The terrain is ideal: rolling sandy land sweeping over slopes well-wooded with umbrella pine. There are holes which border the constantly changing seaside lagoon and marshland bird sanctuary of the Ria Formosa and three real testers which make full use of the inland lake that is a central feature of the property.

The upmarket, controlled development of the Quinta do Lago estate began in 1972, which makes San Lorenzo a comparative newcomer. Yet its gently winding fairways have settled easily into their surroundings and, despite its essentially modern American style, the course owes as much to the original landscape as to the creative hand of the architect.

Property development has been tastefully restrained from affecting the overall sense of peace and green isolation. The most scenically memorable stretch of holes starts at the short (141yd/129m) 5th, where the shot is played

across a deep hollow to a green backed by views of beach and ocean. From here you plunge down a left-hand dogleg par 4 which curves between the pine-clad hillside and the lurking waters of the Ria Formosa. It is immediately followed by another, almost identical, test, with the marshland vista dazzling the eye and water nudging up in front of a shallow green backed with sand. Survive these and the 8th, a mere 574yd/525m from the back markers, awaits. Placement, length, skill and courage are required on this snaking, narrow dogleg left, with water to the right and an inevitably long approach to a semi-island green. Know your game and play within it here for success.

All great courses save the real challenge for the closing holes: never more so than here. In contrast to the 8th, the 17th borders the opposite bank of the lagoon, curving left just 376yd/344m but with water all the way and a sloping fairway with bunkers easing you towards it. The approach must carry a corner of the lagoon to a small green. Then the 18th is a par 4 of 406yd/371m with water up the left-hand side – a classic case of risk and

Above: The approach shot to the island green of the 18th is demanding. Below: Putting on the green of the 422yd/386m 6th hole, with the Ria Formosa beyond.

reward. The island green lies across a neck of water. If you drive left for the ideal approach, you risk the lake; keep right and you have a longer second shot to a shallow, well-bunkered target: unforgettable, whatever your score.

Quinta do Lago

Quinta do Lago Campo de Golfe, Quinta do Lago, 8135
Almancil, Algarve
TEL: (289) 390700 FAX: (289) 394013
LOCATION: 12 miles/20km west of Faro, on Quinta do
Lago estate via Almancil on EN125
COURSE: 18 holes, 7095yd/6488m, par 72, SSS 73
TYPE OF COURSE: Undulating sandy land with umbrella
pines and coastal water
DESIGNER: William Mitchell (1974)
GREEN FEES: EEEE
FACILITIES: Pro shop, cart, trolley and equipment hire,
tuition, putting green, driving range, changing facilities,
roving on-course refreshments, bar and restaurant in
clubhouse, riding, watersports and
tennis nearby
VISITORS: Current handicap certificate required

QUINTA DO LAGO

HOLE	YD	M	PAR	HOLE	YD	M	PAR
1	427	390	4	10	448	410	4
2	547	500	5	11	208	190	3
3	423	387	4	12	503	460	5
4	187	171	3	13	355	325	4
5	552	505	5	14	419	383	4
6	383	350	4	15	219	200	3
7	199	182	3	16	407	372	4
8	421	385	4	17	558	510	5
9	388	355	4	18	451	413	4
OUT	3527	3225	36	IN	3568	3263	36

7095YD • 6488M • PAR 72

Quinta do Lago ('the farm by the lake') was conceived from 1972 by entrepreneur André Jordan as a secluded, upmarket, low-density residential community on gently undulating land, studded with umbrella pines, that led down to the now-protected marshlands of the Ria Formosa lagoon by the sea. The concept called for infrastructure of quality, with sporting and recreational facilities of the highest standard, including several golf courses. Despite the domestic revolution in 1974 and subsequent economic fluctuations, the project has survived almost intact and continues to offer visitors a range of holiday and property opportunities within a context of restrained excellence.

The first Quinta do Lago course (there are now four 18-hole courses on the property, with more planned) was created by William Mitchell in 1974,

making it the first course to be designed by an American in Portugal. The original 18 holes have hosted the Portuguese Open on no less than seven occasions – telling testimony to the quality of what was intended primarily as a holiday resort layout. Two further nine-hole loops were added in later years, all returning to the vicinity of the small but attractive clubhouse, and were for a long time designated as the A, B, C and D nines, allowing a variety of playing combinations (and course maintenance), all par 72. Recently, however, the A and D holes have been redesignated the Ria Formosa course (see next entry) and the longtime championship 18 retained as Quinta do Lago.

Few locations can have been better suited to the creation of vacation golf of the highest quality. The rolling sandy land has a natural covering of umbrella pine, drains well and maintains a diverse flora, including

Ria Formosa
Golf Course

Ria Formosa
Golf Course

Quinta do
Lago Golf
Course

many wild flowers. At one end the holes wind independently through the forested slopes; at the other, the course edges out into the lagoon and the wildlife habitat of the Ria Formosa, easy on the eye but offering opportunities for penal water. The holes show a sympathetic appreciation of the terrain, providing picturesque memories as well as a test of your game. They require a variety of shots, both draw and fade from the tee, have the influence of water on three occasions and include a number of holes that have tested players of the highest calibre.

Three holes on the back nine stand out. The 10th, 448yd/410m, par 4, is a dogleg right with a generous landing area for the straight hitter. The approach, across a valley to a steeply elevated, well-bunkered green, must be up or it will roll back down the slope. The 15th is the hole most visitors remember, if only for the cost in wet golf balls! A daunting 219yd/200m from the back tee and all carry over a lake to the front edge of a green encircled with pines, it demands length and finesse in equal measure. It is very scenic (one for the cameras) but easily underclubbed, especially in a breeze – be warned.

The final hole is suitably testing, as befits a Portuguese Open Championship venue: a long, 451yd/413m dogleg left with a large sandtrap and pines on the angle. Too far right off the tee is in the trees; left demands a long carry. The spacious green, sloping right to left, is well trapped on both sides.

The threatening 15th hole, with its long 219yd/200m water carry, viewed from behind. Finding this very large green does not guarantee two putts.

5 Ria Formosa

*Ria Formosa Golf Course, Quinta do Lago, 8135
Almancil, Algarve*
TEL: *(289) 390700* **FAX:** *(289) 394013*
LOCATION: *12 miles/20km west of Faro, on Quinta do
Lago estate via Almancil on EN125*
COURSE: *18 holes, 6786yd/6205m, par 72, SSS 73*
TYPE OF COURSE: *Undulating sandy land with
established umbrella pines*
DESIGNERS: *William Mitchell, Joseph Lee with Rocky
Roquemore (1974/1989)*
GREEN FEES: *EEEE*
FACILITIES: *Pro shop, cart, trolley and equipment hire,
tuition, putting green, driving range, changing facilities,
roving on-course refreshments, bar and restaurant in
clubhouse; riding, watersports and tennis nearby*
VISITORS: *Current handicap certificate required*

Just because its sibling has hosted the
Portuguese Open, you should not assume
that the 18 holes of Ria Formosa are in any
way inferior. Recently established as a course
in its own right, named after the nearby nature
reserve, it once formed part of the four nine-
hole loops of Quinta do Lago, providing a
variety of interesting and testing combinations.

Although not actually within view of the
coastal wetlands and offering only two water
hazards, it more than compensates with a
succession of demanding doglegs, level
changes and well-protected, often elevated
greens. Also, despite being the product of the
combined American design talents of William
Mitchell, Joseph Lee and Rocky Roquemore,
the course plays as a homogenous whole, its
fairways winding and dipping past clusters of
umbrella pine and strategic sand.

The most visually memorable hole is the
12th, a sharp 395yd/361m left-hand dogleg
around a sizeable lake, the narrow strip of
fairway turning through 90° to a green framed
by three sand traps and water. It pays to be
conservative here, despite the obvious
temptation to get close off the tee. An iron
into play will reap rewards. The course is noted
for its par 5s, none more so than the 11th and
18th. The former winds past strategic clumps
of pine and 11 bunkers, requiring accuracy
rather than length. The latter, 525yd/480m,
offers a water-carry off the tee to a fairway
sloped left towards sand, a second into a deep
valley and the approach up to a sloping,
double-tier green of treacherous reputation.

*Floral attractions at the 401yd/367m 1st hole, which
doglegs gently downhill left around trees to a tilted green,
well protected by sand and hidden from the tee.*

6 *Vale do Lobo: Ocean Course*

Parque de Golfe, 8135-864 Vale do Lobo Codex, Algarve
TEL: *(289) 393939* **FAX:** *(289) 353003*
E-MAIL: *golf@etvdla.pt* **WEB SITE:** *www.valedolobo.pt*
LOCATION: *In Vale do Lobo, 4 miles/6km south-west of Almancil off EN125 west of Faro*
COURSE: *18 holes, 5931yd/5424m, par 71, SSS 71*
TYPE OF COURSE: *Undulating sandy land, flanked by umbrella pines, sloping down to seaside*
DESIGNERS: *Sir Henry Cotton; Pitman & Vansittart (1968/1974)*
GREEN FEES: *EEEE*
FACILITIES: *Pro shop, cart, trolley and equipment hire, tuition, putting and chipping greens, driving range, roving snack buggy on course, changing facilities, bar and restaurant*
VISITORS: *Handicap certificate requested; strict dress code*

Vale do Lobo ('valley of the wolf') opened in 1968 as 18 holes designed by the late Sir Henry Cotton. The back nine of the original course (Orange) form the last nine holes of the Ocean; the other holes are incorporated into the Royal layout. In 1974, a third nine-hole loop (Green) was added, based on the original design of Sir Henry Cotton, and this is now the front nine of the Ocean.

From its inception, Vale do Lobo offered playable golf in a landscape of great natural

Real seaside golf on the edge of the ocean. The 210yd/192m par-3 15th hole is a most attractive test, particularly into a breeze.

beauty. Fairways lined with pine and fig trees merged with pomegranate, olive and orange orchards inland. The slopes spilled gently down to seaside cliffs and a long white beach. It was a world apart, with young caddies in straw hats, an attractive additional nine-hole par-3 layout and an air of relaxed pioneering.

In 1987, the courses came under new ownership and were separated into the Ocean Course and the Royal. The Ocean embodies most of the original spirit of Henry Cotton's concept, upgraded by the American Rocky Roquemore. It combines an attractive setting, blessed with mature umbrella pine and rich flora, plus the hazards of the course itself. Overall, it is the more photogenic of the two layouts in Vale do Lobo, with two holes cascading down to beach-front greens rimmed with palm or pine, plus a genuine links hole beside the sea, 210yd/192m par 3, with out-of-bounds left and two sizeable bunkers guarding its elevated, breeze-affected green.

7 Vale do Lobo: Royal Course

Vale do Lobo Parque do Golfe, 8135-864 Vale do Lobo Codex, Algarve
TEL: *(289) 393939* **FAX:** *(289) 353003*
E-MAIL: *golf@etvdla.pt* **WEB SITE:** *www.valedolobo.pt*
LOCATION: *In Vale do Lobo, 4 miles/6km south-west of Almancil off EN125 west of Faro*
COURSE: *18 holes, 6616yd/6050m, par 72, SSS 72*
TYPE OF COURSE: *Rolling sandy land with mature trees, seafront and several water hazards*
DESIGNERS: *Sir Henry Cotton; Rocky Roquemore (1968/1997)*
GREEN FEES: *EEEEE*
FACILITIES: *Pro shop, cart, trolley and equipment hire, tuition, putting and chipping greens, driving range, roving snack buggy, changing facilities, bar, snack bar and restaurant*
VISITORS: *Handicap certificate required; maximum: men 27, ladies 35; strict dress code*

VALE DO LOBO
ROYAL COURSE

HOLE	YD	M	PAR	HOLE	YD	M	PAR
1	470	430	5	10	361	330	4
2	317	290	4	11	530	485	5
3	427	390	4	12	366	335	4
4	344	315	4	13	399	365	4
5	514	470	5	14	388	355	4
6	432	395	4	15	323	295	4
7	164	150	3	16	224	205	3
8	421	385	4	17	405	370	4
9	169	155	3	18	361	330	4
OUT	3259	2980	36	IN	3357	3070	36

6616 YD • 6050M • PAR 72

Vale do Lobo has a special place in the history of Portuguese golf. Along with Penina and Vilamoura, it was one of the first three 18-hole courses to be opened in the Algarve in the 1960s, forming the vanguard of what has now become a major tourist industry in Portugal. Visitors – mostly from Britain – came on holiday and played the course, told their like-minded friends and the market for winter holiday golf, with all the various related peripheral activities such as real estate development, took off.

Much has happened to the location (and the course) since then: new ownership in 1987, the separation of the original 18-hole course to form parts of two new courses, the Ocean and the Royal (the latter adding nine new holes by the American designer Rocky Roquemore), plus unfettered residential development, have completely changed the face of Vale do Lobo. From a holiday golfer's viewpoint, at least, this has not generally been for the better. Of the original course laid out by Sir Henry Cotton in 1968, only nine holes remain on the Royal, and of these the 6th (now the 15th) hole has been shortened and emasculated to suit a housing project. The new holes of the Royal, which run over slopes further inland, are laid out in typical Roquemore style, with some excellent tests involving water at the 6th and 11th but demonstrating little sympathy for the original course design. The result is something of a salad: overdressed and decidedly overpriced, with the second highest green fee in Portugal.

Golf courses, particularly if they have been well planned, mature into prime versions of the original, with taller trees, better definition and some fine-tuning along the way. Sadly, Vale do Lobo, which was never a layout of great class or quality, has taken a series of steps

Awesome whenever you play it but exceptional in a sea breeze, the 16th hole demands your best shot with both club and camera.

backwards in terms of being a relaxed setting for holiday golf. The caddies and the par-3 course have gone; in their place, the estate has seen continuous, concentrated residential development to become, in effect, a mini-township, a coastal community. What started as vacation golf with some housing has become an urban overdose with golf holes squeezed between.

The courses are there as assets for the resident members; they are over-regulated, pretentious, commercial and restricted for most others. This lost innocence is to some extent offset by elegant course furniture, ornamental gardening and a profusion of flowers and modern statuary around the clubhouse and putting green. However, relaxed it is not; nor, classed against its peers, does it live up to the title 'Royal'.

The star attraction and arguably, over the last 30-odd years, the most photographed hole in Portugal, is the par-3 16th, formerly the 7th on the Yellow nine. This 224yd/205m hole is not totally demanding since, if you do not fancy the carry over the bunker protecting most of the green, there is a shot short right to leave a pitch and putt. The hole is made, however, in the mind. For most of the way, deep ravines of red-ochre cliff face yawn jaggedly up at your ball, while below to the left, a long strand of white beach edging the sea stretches on up to Quarteira. Do take time to admire one of the best seaside golf views in the land, since the shot to follow will take all your concentration.

Future plans include a hotel, another golf course created in 'links' style and nearly 1,000 further housing units. Golf is a subjective experience; only the visitor can decide whether one spectacular hole justifies the hype, cost and essentially formal experience of playing here.

Vila Sol **8**

Golf Vila Sol, Morgadinhos, Alto do Semino, 8125
Quarteira, Algarve
TEL: *(289) 300505* **FAX:** *(289) 300592*
LOCATION: *12 miles/20km west of Faro on EN125, turn
left on N396 for Quarteira*
COURSE: *18 holes, 6854yd/6267m, par 72, SSS 72*
TYPE OF COURSE: *Gently undulating sandy land, densely
forested, with a number of water hazards*
DESIGNER: *Donald Steel (1991)*
GREEN FEES: *EEEE*
FACILITIES: *Pro shop, cart, trolley and equipment hire,
tuition, golf academy with driving range, putting greens, on-
course snacks at 9th hole, changing facilities, bar and
restaurant in clubhouse, nearby tennis and beach club*
VISITORS: *Current handicap certificate required; maximum:
men 27, ladies 35; dress code; soft spikes only*

\multicolumn{7}{c}{VILA SOL}						
HOLE	YD	M	PAR	HOLE	YD	M	PAR
1	417	381	4	10	388	355	4
2	445	407	4	11	499	456	5
3	421	385	4	12	342	313	4
4	208	190	3	13	174	159	3
5	429	392	4	14	553	506	5
6	540	494	5	15	194	177	3
7	197	180	3	16	378	346	4
8	546	499	5	17	404	369	4
9	319	292	4	18	400	366	4
OUT	3522	3220	36	IN	3332	3047	36

6854 YD • 6267M • PAR 72

The first impression of the golf course at Vila Sol is how natural it appears; how little change seems to have been required to the existing landscape. Such thoughts only serve to confirm the design skills of the British architect Donald Steel. This course is a near neighbour to the Old Course at Vilamoura, which is an acknowledged masterpiece by Frank Pennink. With Vila Sol, his first venture in Portugal, Steel has maintained the same philosophy of preserving nature, inheriting the concept of using the land to shape the course, with commendable results.

Opened in 1991, Vila Sol's quality, both of design and maintenance, was recognized with the opportunity to host the Portuguese Open in both 1992 and 1993. The visiting professionals were fulsome in their praise, particularly of the condition of the greens. Carved mainly from dense pine forest which is supplemented by fig, oak and almond trees, the holes require accuracy from the tee with a succession of narrow, tree-lined fairways. Strategic water across the line of play is also a factor, forcing the golfer into important decisions between boldness and discretion. It is a true test of championship quality, despite its holiday location.

One unusual feature is that, whereas with most top courses the degree of difficulty increases through the round, here the examination begins on the first tee and presents the player with four extremely demanding holes from the start. The 1st, 417yd/381m par 4, would serve as an excellent finishing hole rather than an opener (see page 55). Effectively straight, with just a touch of left turn near the green, the tilted fairway throws every shot left, where a number of strategic pines – which includes one guarding the green – come into play. Trees edge out from the right to keep the approach honest to a green built as an elevated shelf protected by a large bunker on the right corner. The next two holes are equally demanding, at 445yd/407m and

421yd/385m respectively, especially as they run in opposing directions. A telling factor is that these three starting holes rank 3, 9 and 1 on the scorecard index. Then the 4th runs 208yd/190m from an elevated tee across a dip to a large, equally elevated green, once again guarded by a solitary but highly strategic pine.

Master the opening stretch and the rest of the course, although tight and testing, must appear easier. However, you must keep your eye on the water hazards, which lurk at inconvenient distances either off the tee or on the approach, especially at the par-3 7th, where the stroke must carry all the way to the well-protected, two-level green, which slopes alarmingly back towards the water.

The 18th hole finishes just below the timbered clubhouse terrace, which offers an excellent view, both for casual drinkers and for serious clients of the excellent restaurant. Restricted property development has been discreet and mostly away from the golf course, an environmental policy which brought a Green Flag award to the club in 1996. A further nine holes are planned.

Above: The 15th is a fine par 3 of 194yd/177m, typical of the terrain at Vila Sol. Below: The sunken green of the 400yd/366m 18th lies right below the popular clubhouse terrace.

9 Vilamoura: The Old Course

The Old Course, Clube de Golfe Vilamoura, Vilamoura,
8125 Quarteira, Algarve
TEL: (289) 310341 FAX: (289) 310321
LOCATION: 12 miles/20km west of Faro on EN125,
turning left for Quarteira
COURSE: 18 holes, 6839yd/6254m, par 73, SSS 72
TYPE OF COURSE: Undulating sandy land with
umbrella pines
DESIGNERS: Frank Pennink (1969)
GREEN FEES: EEEEE
FACILITIES: Pro shop, cart, trolley and equipment hire,
tuition, driving range and putting green, changing facilities,
bar and restaurant
VISITORS: Handicap certificate required; maximum: men
24, ladies 28; soft spikes only

VILAMOURA
THE OLD COURSE

HOLE	YD	M	PAR	HOLE	YD	M	PAR
1	339	310	4	10	167	153	3
2	476	435	5	11	427	390	4
3	354	324	4	12	533	487	5
4	178	163	3	13	380	348	4
5	530	485	5	14	481	440	5
6	232	212	3	15	164	150	3
7	430	393	4	16	562	514	5
8	458	419	4	17	386	353	4
9	290	265	5	18	452	413	4
OUT	3287	3006	36	IN	3552	3248	37

6839YD • 6254M • PAR 73

The common thread of history provides both benchmark and background to the unfolding, ever-changing world of resort golf. However, it is rare for an earlier course to stand the test of time. One that does, and which remains arguably the best and fairest test of the game in Portugal, is the classic layout of the Old Course at Vilamoura. Created in a setting of great natural charm, its strategic challenge is wholly due to the understanding, foresight and skill of its British architect, Frank Pennink.

At the time of its inception in 1969, the course at Vilamoura was one of three in the central Algarve region which marked the start of the tourist revolution: the creation of modern resort courses initially in the south of Portugal and later throughout the country. The quality of its design, a genuine test from the back tees but highly playable from the marks of the day, proved popular both with amateur visitors and with the professionals who played in the

Algarve and Portuguese Opens held there, as well as the World Ladies Team Championship, won by the United States in 1976.

Well aware of the technical improvements in course construction and maintenance which have occurred during the 30 years following the creation of the Old Course, the new owners of the Vilamoura complex (which now totals 63 holes in play with more courses planned) called in another leading British golf architect, Martin Hawtree.

He has overseen the construction of new tees, fairways and greens to the highest specification, while sympathetically retaining most of the original Pennink design. The result is a triumph: a classic test, reminiscent of many pine-lined courses in southern England, with fairways sweeping around and over a central hill past dense clusters of umbrella pine, all kept in superb condition.

The most memorable features of the Old Course are the narrow chutes of pine, funnelling down from the tees to distant velvet fairways, and the four highly demanding short

The short 4th presents a testing shot over water and sand to an elevated green. It is at its toughest when the pin is set on the right and the umbrella pines come into play.

holes. Ranging in length from 164 to 232yd/150 to 212m, each presents a totally different examination, each demanding a precise, well-judged shot for success. They are also the most attractive holes on the course.

The Old Course is not long by modern standards. Its charms lie rather in its subtlety, its natural unmanufactured beauty and its enduring status as a true test of the game. To play here is a privilege; to play well here is a bonus to be treasured for many years to come.

A feature of courses created by Frank Pennink, of which Portugal can offer four, is the way the slightly off-line drive, still well within the fairway, is blocked in its route to the green by a single tree or extended branch. Wide fairways offer inviting targets, yet only the perfect line will open up the easier second

shot. Strategy and a clear understanding of your own abilities are essential for success.

In tandem with the renewal of the Old Course, a fine clubhouse has been erected close to the first tee. In single-storey, rustic elegance, it captures the spirit of the course, offering high standards of cuisine and service against a background of relaxed, understated comfort.

MASTER OF THE NATURAL CHALLENGE

J. J. F. Pennink was an outstanding amateur golfer, winner of the English title twice and a Walker Cup player. He brought vast experience, both as a player and an administrator, to his work as a golf course architect, adding a flair for design and a sympathy with nature. He has left a lasting legacy around the world of the art of using the natural lie of the land to test a golfer's skills. His work in Portugal includes Vilamoura, Palmares, Aroeira and Vimeiro.

10 *Vilamoura: Pinhal Course*

Pinhal Golf Course, Vilamoura, 8125 Quarteira, Algarve
TEL: *(289) 310390* **FAX:** *(289) 310393*
LOCATION: *See the Old Course (page 34)*
COURSE: *18 holes, 6787yd/6206m, par 72, SSS 71*
TYPE OF COURSE: *Mixture of tight pine-lined holes and open, rolling terrain*
DESIGNERS: *Frank Pennink (1976); Robert Trent Jones; Martin Hawtree*
GREEN FEES: *EEE*
FACILITIES: *Pro shop, club, cart and trolley hire, practice ground, putting green, changing facilities, bar and restaurant in clubhouse*
VISITORS: *Handicap certificate required; maximum: men 28, ladies 36*

If the Pinhal course could be said to offer any special quality, it is variety, both in terms of design and playing quality. It started life as the second course at Vilamoura, designed by Frank Pennink in 1976, with fairways winding narrowly through a sloping forest of dense umbrella pine. Since then, the demands of property development and related matters have led to both the

The 381yd/348m 4th at Pinhal, although not long, demands accurate placement from the tee and a precise approach over water to a well-bunkered green.

relocation and redesign of many holes, primarily under the label of Robert Trent Jones and, most recently, Martin Hawtree. The result is a course of varying character – even split personality – with open, rolling, mounded American-style holes annexed to those of the original, traditional woodland course. Barely half of the original Pennink holes remain, scant testimony to the subtle genius of a very British golf architect.

The best of these are the 2nd, a narrowing dogleg right of 435yd/398m with a solitary fairway pine positioned to block out less than perfect drives, and the 3rd, a double-dogleg 550yd/503m par 5, which offers a challenging tee shot over trees to find the open route to the green, or strategic placement for a more conventional approach. The discreet clubhouse, which looks out over a large driving range, offers a good snack menu and a relaxed ambience.

11 *Vilamoura: Laguna Course*

Laguna Golf Course, Vilamoura, 8125 Quarteira, Algarve
TEL: *(289) 310180* **FAX:** *(289) 310183*
LOCATION: *See the Old Course (page 34)*
COURSE: *18 holes, 6707yd/6133m, par 72 SSS 73*
TYPE OF COURSE: *Combination of heathland, lake holes and marsh areas near the sea*
DESIGNERS: *Joseph Lee; Rocky Roquemore (1990/1993)*
GREEN FEES: *EEE*
FACILITIES: *Pro shop, club, cart and trolley hire, driving range, putting green, changing facilities, bar and restaurant in clubhouse and on terrace*
VISITORS: *Handicap certificate required; maximum: men 28, ladies 36*

Third of the golfing developments on the Vilamoura estate, Laguna has evolved from being part of three interlinked nine-hole courses, two in play from 1990, the other from 1993. All were the work of the American designers, Joseph Lee and Rocky Roquemore. The first loop, previously known as the North and laid out over rolling heathland, was absorbed into the new Millennium Course, which opened in May 2000. The remaining 18 holes, the East and the South, now form Laguna.

The course combines some highly strategic holes, requiring accuracy and restraint in equal measure, with areas bordering the wetlands towards the marina. Here, seaside characteristics and vast areas of sand and water dictate play. Sparse rough, few trees, bare areas of sandy soil and an ever-present breeze contribute to the coastal feel of this section.

Two pairs of holes should be treated with the utmost respect. The 4th and 5th, a 220yd/201m par 3 and 344yd/315m par 4, navigate two sides of a lake, the latter hole extremely narrowly. On the back nine, the 14th and 15th are card-wreckers. The 14th, 378yd/346m, has a narrow curving fairway and challenging second, bringing water into play throughout. A great drive is needed at the 554yd/507m 15th, with water bisecting the fairway and affecting subsequent shots. The Moorish domed clubhouse has been expanded, offering excellent facilities for both the Laguna and Millennium courses.

An Algarve chimney tee-marker guards the Laguna course's treacherous par-3 4th – all carry, with water right, to a steeply sloping green.

12. Pine Cliffs

Sheraton Algarve Pine Cliffs, Praia da Falésia, P.O. Box 644, 8200 Albufeira, Algarve
TEL: *(289) 500100* **FAX:** *(289) 500117*
LOCATION: *22 miles/35km west of Faro off EN125 between Vilamoura and Açoteias*
COURSE: *9 holes, 2487yd/2274m, par 33/66, SSS 67*
TYPE OF COURSE: *Gently sloping clifftop land*
DESIGNER: *Martin Hawtree (1991)*
GREEN FEES: *9 holes EE; 18 holes EEE*
FACILITIES: *Pro shop, trolley and equipment hire, tuition in comprehensive academy with target-green driving range, chipping and putting greens, changing facilities, bar, café and restaurant in hotel complex*
VISITORS: *Current handicap certificate required; maximum: men and ladies 36; strict dress code*

This nine-hole course was built in 1991 for clients of the Sheraton Algarve hotel, but is worth a visit. It is a shortish, interesting mixture of holes over gently sloping land blessed with a number of mature trees.

However you play the earlier holes, the 9th, called the 'Devil's Parlour', is unforgettable, and one of the most recognized in Portugal. From a diminutive eyrie of a back tee, perched high above the jagged red ochre of the cliff face, this 224yd/205m par 3 demands a heroic carry over the fearsome void to reach the narrow green nestling snugly under the hotel. One of the more spectacular short holes in golf, it is reminiscent of the 17th at Cypress Point.

The academy has a practice area to die for, with exact distances to nine target greens; some are bunkered, and all are turfed and mown identically to the course itself. It is popular with wintering tour players.

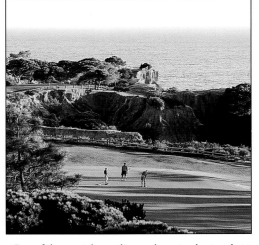

One of the most demanding and spectacular tee-shots in the whole of Portugal. The 9th at Pine Cliffs viewed from behind.

13. Salgados

Salgados Golf Club, Apartado 2266, Vale do Rabelho, 8200 Albufeira, Algarve
TEL: *(289) 591111* **FAX:** *(289) 591112*
LOCATION: *5 miles/8km west of Albufeira off EN125 between Faro and Portimão*
COURSE: *18 holes, 6649yd/6080m, par 72, SSS 72*
TYPE OF COURSE: *Coastal marshland with much water*
DESIGNERS: *Pedro de Vasconcelos, Robert Muir-Graves (1994)*
GREEN FEES: *EEE*
FACILITIES: *Pro shop, cart, trolley and equipment hire, tuition, driving range, chipping and putting greens, changing facilities, bar and restaurant in clubhouse*
VISITORS: *Handicap certificate required; maximum: men 28, ladies 36*

Sited centrally in the Algarve, Salgados, opened in 1994, offers a complete contrast to most courses in this region. On a level site by the sea, bordered on one side by sand dunes and by a marshland wildfowl sanctuary on the other, it is virtually treeless, with links-style holes flanked in almost every case by water. The succession of saltwater lagoons, canals and freshwater lakes appears to cover as much of the area as the course which navigates it. Salgados is a fine test of shotmaking, especially in any kind of breeze.

With its narrow fairways, gently mounded greens and hazards, it puts a premium on club selection. Its lush turf is watered using an eco-friendly system that supplies recycled waste water. The best hole is the 6th, a narrowing 563yd/ 515m dogleg, where the approach must carry across a lake to a green backed by ancient olive trees. Take plenty of balls.

14 Vale de Milho

Vale de Milho Golfe, Apartado 1273, Praia do Carvoeiro, 8400 Lagoa, Algarve
TEL: *(282) 358502* **FAX:** *(282) 358497*
E-MAIL: *gericontroi@mail.telepac.pt*
LOCATION: *2 miles/3km east of Carvoeiro, south of Lagoa on EN125, 6 miles/9km east of Portimão*
COURSE: *9 holes (2 sets of tees), 2018yd/1845m, par 54, SSS 54*
TYPE OF COURSE: *Genuine par-3 layout over sloping ground with mature trees*
DESIGNER: *Dave Thomas (1990)*
GREEN FEES: *9 holes E; 18 holes EE*
FACILITIES: *Pro shop, trolley and equipment hire, teaching academy, putting and chipping greens, changing facilities, bar and restaurant in clubhouse*
VISITORS: *Knowledge of golf and etiquette required*

Amid all the championship challenges for which the Algarve is internationally famous, Vale de Milho represents a peaceful backwater, an unpretentious but very attractive short course that sets out to be nothing else. Ryder Cup player Dave Thomas has produced a pleasant layout over a fairly steeply sloping site, with nine holes which range from 66yd/60m to 179yd/164m. Using alternate sets of tees, the course can be played as 18 holes. The designer has ensured full-size greens and some strategic water. The course is an excellent examination of your short game, as well as being a good baptism for new players. The inevitable property development is not too obtrusive. The extremely spacious clubhouse has a large elevated terrace where you can enjoy a post-round drink while getting an excellent view of several of the holes.

The view from the clubhouse balcony of the 2nd green at Vale de Milho, a 179yd/164m par 3 that presents a narrow target.

15 Gramacho

Pestana Golf – Gramacho Course, Apartado 1011, 8400-908 Carvoeiro, Lagoa, Algarve
TEL: *(282) 340900* **FAX:** *(282) 340901*
E-MAIL: *g.pestana@telepac.pt*
WEB SITE: *www.pestana.com*
LOCATION: *Next to Vale da Pinta Course near Carvoeiro, south of Lagoa on EN125, 6 miles/9km east of Portimão*
COURSE: *18 holes, 6473yd/5919m, par 72, SSS 71*
TYPE OF COURSE: *Rolling sandy land with olive trees, old walls and lakes*
DESIGNER: *Ronald Fream (1991)*
GREEN FEES: *EEE (18 holes)*
FACILITIES: *Pro shop, cart, trolley and equipment hire, David Leadbetter teaching academy, driving range, putting green, changing facilities, bar and restaurant in clubhouse*
VISITORS: *Maximum handicap 36 for both men and ladies*

Gramacho embodies a totally new concept that hotels and other developers with limited available land might well consider. Ronald Fream has created a full 18-hole course on space suitable for only nine holes, by using the fairways twice but from alternate angles. With totally different teeing areas and 18 full-size greens, players get contrasting holes to play the second time around. With deep understanding and a wealth of experience, Fream has achieved a successful course that will appeal to good players as well as novices. It has enough length for anyone playing off the back tees but can also encourage lesser lights into the game.

A new clubhouse with a pool, two tennis courts and lawn bowls opened in January 2000. In due course, an additional nine will extend the Gramacho concept over 36 holes.

16 *Vale da Pinta*

Pestana Golf – Pinta Course, Apartado 1011, 8400-908 Carvoeiro, Lagoa, Algarve
TEL: *(282) 340900* **FAX:** *(282) 340901*
E-MAIL: *g.pestana@mail.telepac.pt*
WEB SITE: *www.pestana.com*
LOCATION: *Next to Gramacho Course near Carvoeiro, south of Lagoa on EN125, 6 miles/9km east of Portimão*
COURSE: *18 holes, 6727yd/6151m, par 71, SSS 72*
TYPE OF COURSE: *Rolling slopes dotted with mature trees and strategic lakes*
DESIGNER: *Ronald Fream (1992)*
GREEN FEES: *EEE*
FACILITIES: *Pro shop, cart, trolley and equipment hire, David Leadbetter teaching academy, driving range, putting and chipping greens, changing facilities, bar and restaurant in clubhouse*
VISITORS: *Handicap certificate required; maximum: men 27, ladies 35*

VALE DA PINTA

HOLE	YD	M	PAR	HOLE	YD	M	PAR
1	348	318	4	10	418	382	4
2	389	356	4	11	178	163	3
3	394	360	4	12	534	488	5
4	560	512	5	13	367	336	4
5	184	168	3	14	525	480	5
6	449	411	4	15	196	179	3
7	201	184	3	16	353	323	4
8	366	335	4	17	221	202	3
9	408	373	4	18	635	581	5
OUT	3299	3017	35	IN	3427	3134	36

6727YD • 6151M • PAR 71

Pinta remains one of Portugal's great unrecognized jewels, a fine test of golf in an undisturbed rural Algarvian locale. Created by Ronald Fream in 1992, it flows over and down a series of tree-encrusted hills and valleys in majestic fashion, posing its subtle problems with great charm. Clusters of almond, fig, carob and olive trees abound, the latter in many cases between 400 and 600 years old, with one ancient specimen on the 18th hole reckoned to have survived for 1,200 years. The architect must have felt the hand of God on this landscape; his lakes, mounded greens and large bunkers blend into the natural setting in timeless

fashion, with fine views from the higher ground to the Monchique mountains and, so far, unblemished by property development.

The course, which is kept in excellent condition, has recently reverted to the original sequence of holes, starting at the highest central point where the new clubhouse is sited. Pinta, along with the Gramacho layout next to it, is owned by the Pestana Group, Portugal's largest hoteliers with 22 hotels, five of which are in the immediate area. There are considerable investment plans for the course and the back tees are already being extended to create a genuine championship examination of 7357yd/6727m.

Selecting the best or most memorable holes on this course poses problems, for all have their distinct claims and there are no easy pars. The 3rd hole (see page 52) is a classic risk-and-reward par 4, offering plenty of space for a safe downhill shot right, followed by a demanding second, or the alternative – risking all over a dogleg infested with trees, sand and scrub to leave a simple pitch. The 4th hole, at 560yd/512m, is the first par 5 and requires three thoughtful shots. The drive

The 7th is a spectacular hole played across a valley to a green set into the hillside. It is all carry of 201yd/184m over oceans of sand.

must be straight, between right-hand rough and out-of-bounds, while the narrowing downhill second must avoid strategic sand on a full shot. The well-bunkered, twin-level green, across a small depression, is treacherously fast.

The 7th, 201yd/184m par 3, is a great hole across a natural valley, its mass of protective sand at front and rear dominating the hillside and putting pressure on good club selection. Turning for home, three holes stand out. The 13th is all about position and belies its relatively short length of 367yd/336m. The direct drive on this slight dogleg left must carry water and a large bunker beyond it. There is room to the right but it increases the problems in holding a contoured, elevated, well-protected green off a sloping lie. Shortly

after this, you face the par-3 15th, downhill from a very raised tee open to any breeze, with out-of-bounds close down the right-hand side of the deep but narrow green and a sea of sand to carry.

It has been said many times that great courses always have fine finishes, and Pinta is no exception. The 17th, 221yd/202m par 3, is played downhill to an angled, shallow green totally protected from the front by a large area of sand and with trees behind. The last provides a great closing test, snaking 635yd/581m past huddles of ancient olive trees. Three very good shots are required to avoid well-placed sand and strategically sited trees, and to hold the narrow fairway. The approach, which may well require quite a long club, is to a small, two-tier green, and a par here will have been truly earned. This is a great course which is still something of an undiscovered secret and is very worthy of holding a top event in the future.

17 Penina

*Le Meridien-Penina Golf & Resort, P. O. Box 146,
8501-952 Portimão Codex, Algarve*
TEL: *(282) 420200* **FAX:** *(282) 420300*
LOCATION: *3 miles/5km west of Portimão on EN125.*
COURSES: *Championship 18 holes, 6860yd/6273m,
par 73, SSS 73; Resort 9 holes 3267yd/2987m,
par 35, SSS 71; Academy 9 holes, 2226yd/2035m,
par 30*
TYPE OF COURSE: *Flat former rice paddy with mature
eucalyptus and palm plus much strategic water*
DESIGNER: *Sir Henry Cotton (1966/1972/1977)*
GREEN FEES: *Championship EEEE; Resort (18 holes)
EEE; Academy (18 holes) EE. Lower rates for Meridien
guests*
FACILITIES: *Pro shop, cart, trolley and equipment hire,
tuition, driving range, putting and chipping greens, changing
facilities, roving bar on course, on-site 5-star Meridien Hotel
has swimming pool, tennis, bars and restaurants*
VISITORS: *Handicap certificate required for Championship
Course; maximum: men 28, ladies 36; soft spikes only. No
handicap needed for other courses*

PENINA CHAMPIONSHIP COURSE

HOLE	YD	M	PAR	HOLE	YD	M	PAR
1	445	407	4	10	545	498	5
2	424	388	4	11	540	494	5
3	335	306	4	12	421	385	4
4	386	353	4	13	202	185	3
5	493	451	5	14	391	358	4
6	193	176	3	15	329	301	4
7	339	310	4	16	210	192	3
8	187	171	3	17	521	476	5
9	422	386	4	18	477	436	5
OUT	3224	2948	35	IN	3636	3325	38

6860YD • 6273M • PAR 73

The first three golf courses built in the Algarve were all by British designers, all laid out in the 1960s, and two of them bore the imprint of T. H. Cotton.

Now known as the Henry Cotton Championship Course, the main 18 holes at Penina provide probably the most demanding test of a player's skills (particularly from the extreme back tee measurement of 7042yd/6439m) in the Algarve, if not in Portugal. Dead flat, with the inevitable difficulty that such terrain creates with club selection, the holes are crossed and flanked by a series of streams, ditches and water hazards, demanding precisely executed shots to avoid trouble and achieve par. The course is beautifully maintained, winding past tall stands of eucalyptus and clumps of palm to mainly elevated greens which have subtle slopes and sometimes treacherous speeds.

There is little doubt of the substantial

The first resort golf course built in Portugal in the modern era was the Championship Course at Penina, in 1966. Three times British Open champion, the late Sir Henry Cotton was encouraged to visit and lay out a course over a former rice field just west of Portimão. On an unpromising, wet, treeless site, Cotton grasped the opportunity to renew the British connection with golf in the country that had been established in the 19th century. In the process, he created his masterpiece, a fitting epitaph to one of Britain's most successful professional players and a course which has already hosted a number of Portuguese Open and other championships.

contributions made by Cotton to his profession, to the modern game and the concept of resort golf (see page 44). He was certainly the most successful British professional player of his era. As a golf course architect, however, he has had his critics. In the case of Penina, perhaps, the course shows his apparent inability to see the game from the standpoint of the high-handicapper or beginner and make alternative provision. Consequently, it poses a genuine challenge for players of the very highest calibre while remaining somewhat beyond the capabilities of most.

This elegant resort, with its large centrally sited hotel, does however provide two golfing alternatives. The Resort Course, a more recent nine holes on the north side of the EN125, is less strategically demanding, while the Academy Course, laid out within the

A fine view from the rear of the dogleg par-5 5th hole. It needs two well-struck shots for a comfortable approach over the penal water.

Championship Course, is an interesting 'executive' shortish nine holes par 30.

On level land that had previously been used as a rice field, drainage was always going to be a problem. Considerable efforts have been made in recent years to upgrade and refine certain technical aspects, such as irrigation, and to improve drainage on the fairways. The results make Penina one of the best-kept resort facilities in Europe – difficult to score on but a treat to play.

Two holes show how important strategic water can be. The 5th doglegs left for 493yd/451m, with three bunkers and lateral water to the right plus out-of-bounds following the treeline on the left all the way to the green. Its double-tiered, angled surface lies beyond a substantial lake, putting pressure on the second shot into a narrow funnel of fairway. The 202yd/185m 13th (see page 54) requires a long carry over water, the curving shape of the left-hand fairway, with out-of-bounds on both sides, encouraging the shot to deviate right into the hazard.

Henry Cotton – Maestro

Just as the British introduced golf to Portugal in 1890, so much of the development of the modern game in Europe, from professional tournaments to amateur holiday golf, owes a considerable debt to the life of one quite remarkable Englishman – the late Sir Henry Cotton. An individual in every sense and a man ahead of his time, he spent only the latter part of his career in Portugal, but his contribution to the growth of holiday golf was significant.

Henry Cotton, born in 1907, lived through an important period in the transition of golf into its modern form and, through the fortunate combination of a middle-class public school upbringing and a unique obsession with perfection of performance, he was able to prove an articulate influence on the game. A self-made player, he bridged the gap between the eras of hickory and steel, playing with such heroes as Harry Vardon, James Braid, J. H. Taylor, Walter Hagen, Tommy Armour and Bobby Jones, and determined to fashion himself into a champion.

He entered the game at a time when professionals 'knew their place' and tournament purses were few and small. With single-minded determination, he raised professional standards in dress, status, contracts and levels of play, becoming an international figurehead for the European game, at ease with kings and millionaires, and an outspoken

Always a competitor, Sir Henry Cotton playing a few holes at Penina with the author in 1969.

advocate of practice, technique, fitness and, above all, progress. A pioneer throughout his career, he was among the first to visit and compete seriously in the USA, to elevate the game in Europe and in South America and to occupy an overseas club appointment, at Royal Waterloo in Belgium. He was happy 'to be seen to try to achieve his best and to win' – sporting heresy at the time in Britain.

Henry Cotton was a truly remarkable man. Plagued by ill-health throughout his career, he took the work ethic to extremes. He was also an innovator and an enthusiast for all aspects of golf, forever young at heart. As he put it, 'Youth is not a time of life – it is a state of mind.' The pinnacle of his playing career was to win the British Open on three occasions. In 1934 this included a second round of 65, so remarkable at the time that Dunlop named their leading golf ball after it. He won again in 1937 and – after enforced wartime absence – at Carnoustie in 1948, aged 41.

But his talents encompassed so much more. Always an advocate of strong hands and arms, his search for playing perfection led to his creation of new teaching methods, including the car tyre drill. He wrote numerous books and articles and even moved on into golf architecture. His design concepts enrich five courses in Portugal, where he remained at his masterpiece, Penina, as a respected guru and influence on the game, for the rest of his life.

Alto Golf

*Alto Golf & Country Club, Quinta do Alto do Poco,
Apartado 1, 8501-906 Alvor, Algarve*
TEL: *(282) 416913* **FAX:** *(282) 401046*
E-MAIL: *directors@altoclub.com*
LOCATION: *3 miles/4km west of Portimão on road from
Praia da Rocha to Alvor*
COURSE: *18 holes, 6698yd/6125m, par 72, SSS 73*
TYPE OF COURSE: *Rolling parkland with many trees and
elevated greens*
DESIGNER: *Sir Henry Cotton (1991)*
GREEN FEES: *EEE*
FACILITIES: *Pro shop, cart, trolley and equipment
hire, tuition, driving range, chipping and putting
greens, changing facilities, bar and restaurant
in clubhouse.*
VISITORS: *Current handicap certificate required*

The Alto Golf & Country Club has
remained in the shadow of its near
neighbour Penina since its inception; rather
unfairly, perhaps, since it offers very playable
golf in a relaxed setting. Created from a
preliminary plan by the late Sir Henry
Cotton, the rolling slopes of the Alto Club lie
just inland from the Alvor beachfront
enclosed by the inevitable rise of property
development. That apart, the course has
become well established in the years since it
opened in 1991. Trees have now grown and
delineated the narrow, often doglegged
fairways and the mostly elevated greens.

Laid out over two separate areas of sloping
land, which were always short of space
comfortably to accommodate 18 holes, the
course offers pleasant, if unspectacular,
parkland golf kept in excellent condition,
that can appeal to a broad range of handicaps.
Visitors should, however, be aware that, on
the majority of holes, tight driving lines past
ranks of bushy pine put a premium on
accuracy over length. Many holes rise to an
elevated hilltop green, which affects club
selection but offers the bonus of some fine
inland views.

Alto has two other claims to fame. It lies
near the long-extinct site of the Algarve's first
golf course, a rudimentary sand-green nine
holes dating from the 1920s. It also boasts one
of the longest holes in European golf – the
661yd/604m par-5 16th, where a visitor's
birdie wins a prize. The comfortable timber
clubhouse has excellent terrace views over
much of the back nine.

*Putting on the elevated green of the 478yd/437m par-5
5th hole, one of several with an uphill approach.*

19 *Palmares*

*Palmares Golf, Meia Praia, Apartado 74, 8601-901
Lagos, Algarve*
TEL: *(282) 762953* **FAX:** *(282) 762534*
LOCATION: *At Meia Praia, off EN125 4 miles/6km
north-east of Lagos*
COURSE: *18 holes, 6521yd/5961m, par 71, SSS 72*
TYPE OF COURSE: *Combination of sloping hillside and
links holes by the sea*
DESIGNER: *Frank Pennink (1975)*
GREEN FEES: *EEE*
FACILITIES: *Golf shop, cart, trolley and equipment hire,
professional tuition, driving range, pitching and putting
greens, changing facilities, bar and restaurant in clubhouse*
VISITORS: *Current handicap certificate required*

PALMARES

HOLE	YD	M	PAR	HOLE	YD	M	PAR
1	457	418	4	10	181	165	3
2	351	321	4	11	296	271	4
3	314	287	4	12	437	400	4
4	155	142	3	13	422	386	4
5	602	550	5	14	380	347	4
6	376	344	4	15	232	212	3
7	505	462	5	16	457	418	4
8	155	142	3	17	501	458	5
9	347	317	4	18	351	321	4
OUT	3262	2983	36	IN	3257	2978	35

6519YD • 5961M • PAR 71

The playing of some courses is an achievement; some are a challenge and some, perhaps, rate as holiday souvenirs, but probably no other course engenders the same continuing affection and respect as Palmares. Open since 1975, it was designed by the talented and versatile English architect, Frank Pennink, whose achievements at Vilamoura Old Course (1969) and Aroeira (1972) rank among the best in the country, if not in Europe.

Sited above and along the beach from Meia Praia, it combines great golf with, arguably, some of the best views of any course in Portugal. It also benefits from a continuity of management and considerate service plus the quality of design, as fresh and interesting today as when the course was first opened.

In play for more than a quarter of a century, Palmares blends easily into its rural seaside environment, offering wonderful vistas of the coastline around the Bay of Lagos and, from the higher ground, the mountains of the Monchique inland. The location presented Pennink with a unique situation – a hilltop dotted with flowering shrubs, almond and acacia trees, cascading down to a sandy stretch of linksland with dunes bordering the sea. He grasped the challenge of combining links with parkland golf and produced a truly interesting course of wide variety, that never ceases to charm and challenge. The spectacular views come as a natural bonus.

The special situation of Palmares means that it offers not only holes of two quite distinct types but two separate golfing locations, joined by a steep hillside. In effect, this gives the player three types of terrain to negotiate. By the sea, the five links holes wind past stretches of sand, scrub and dune open to any sea breeze. On the hillside, six steeply sloped fairways link the course to its upper level. Finally, six relatively level parkland holes ease past ancient almond trees, which annually cover the area with a carpet of white blossom. All have greens of high quality.

A round here is as much about taking in the views as mastering the course. The 1st is a tempting opener of 457yd/418m, which plunges downhill in a right-hand dogleg. Length, surprisingly, is not the problem; it is getting the correct line off the tee past tall pines. Whatever the result, pause to take in the panorama of the lower linksland holes and the sea. The other great viewpoint is from the 17th tee. Here, the 501yd/458m par 5 curves downhill to the left and provides the player with a superb vista over the Bay of Lagos, and the urbanization of Alvor, plus a temptation to try to carry the corner over scrubland and trees, a bold line fraught with danger.

The toughest hole is the par-5 5th, which stretches 602yd/550m from the back tee, a long green serpent bordered by a bare sandbank right and sandy scrubland left. Two career shots are needed to have any sight of the small elevated green tucked around the corner to the right, protected by trees and a single bunker; into any sort of wind, a killer.

Superb views are a feature, whether over the 9th green (above) to the Bay of Lagos or (below) across the 16th green to the distant Monchique Hills.

Future plans include resiting the restaurant to offer unrestricted views over the course, a further nine holes and a centrally sited hotel.

20 *Parque da Floresta*

Parque da Floresta Golf & Leisure Resort, Budens, 8650-060 Vila do Bispo, Algarve
TEL: *(282) 690054* **FAX:** *(282) 695157*
LOCATION: *10 miles/16km west of Lagos on EN125, turning right just beyond Budens*
COURSE: *18 holes, 6201yd/5670m, par 72, SSS 72*
TYPE OF COURSE: *Rolling course laid out over often severely sloped hillsides and valleys*
DESIGNER: *Pepe Gancedo (1987)*
GREEN FEES: *EEE*
FACILITIES: *Pro shop, cart, trolley and equipment hire, teaching academy, driving range, pitching and putting greens, changing facilities, bar and à la carte restaurant in clubhouse, on-site spa, tennis, lawn bowls and archery*
VISITORS: *Knowledge of golf and etiquette required; dress code; soft spikes only*

PARQUE DA FLORESTA

HOLE	YD	M	PAR	HOLE	YD	M	PAR
1	341	312	4	10	488	446	5
2	373	341	4	11	152	139	3
3	172	157	3	12	435	398	5
4	495	453	5	13	519	475	5
5	123	112	3	14	425	389	4
6	392	358	4	15	170	155	3
7	197	180	3	16	296	271	4
8	319	292	4	17	416	380	4
9	530	485	5	18	358	327	4
OUT	2942	2690	35	IN	3259	2980	37

6201YD • 5670M • PAR 72

Chemistry has a large part to play in creative expression, and at Parque da Floresta it could hardly have worked better. Pepe Gancedo, a former Spanish amateur champion and the flamboyant designer of some exciting, confrontational courses, such as Torrequebrada in the Costa del Sol, was presented with a wildly extravagant landscape of steep hills and valleys clothed with trees and scrub at the far western end of the Algarve, with some of the finest views anywhere on the coast.

They were made for each other. The result was the 'course of your wildest dreams': provocative, audacious, challenging, difficult, demanding – a layout which initially, in 1987, was dismissed by many as a course too far, not easy to reach and unplayable by most.

So it might have remained, a curiosity for tigers and masochists, until the British-owned Vigia group came along in the early 1990s and saw greater potential in the region as a whole, far beyond the course itself. Experienced in Algarve living, they have invested heavily to create a viable community of discreetly sited housing, supported by a wealth of leisure facilities including a complete health spa, gymnasium, tennis, lawn bowls, archery and much more. Improvements included a major upgrading of the golf course in 1998, in the course of which certain holes were made a touch more playable for the majority. The alterations entailed shortening the first hole to 341yd/312m to make a still daunting but reachable par 4 around an abyss; new greens at the 4th and 5th; work on the fairway of the 10th; a new green at the extended 13th (now par 5) down a curving mountain valley; and a water hazard in front of the all-carry 15th. Above all, the 14th was totally redesigned, creating a great new hole along the valley floor – a tough, narrow 425yd/389m with little room for error from

tee to green. The result is a course which, while retaining its dramatic terrain, is infinitely more playable. Use of a golf buggy is recommended.

Two holes stand out as fine tests, contrasting in length. The 5th hole is one of the shortest in European golf, yet is arguably one of the more difficult, proving the point that length is not everything. From the raised back tee, the small green lies 123yd/112m way below on the bald crest of a steeply sloped mound, ringed by a tree and four bunkers. In any breeze this is a most demanding shot, with severe punishment downhill on all sides.

The other outstanding hole is the 14th, completely resited and converted from one that was palpably unfair into possibly the best on the course. It threads along a tight valley floor, with trouble both sides, to a multi-sloped green set beyond a narrow, well-

The tee-shot view down to the 'postage stamp' 5th hole, just 123yd/112m but open to cross winds and perilous. The uphill approach to the 9th hole can be seen beyond, as can the bowling greens and golf academy.

protected neck of fairway. Fraught with problems, dealing with the 14th is a clear case of knowing your game and playing the hole one shot at a time.

Residential development is in limited hilltop clusters, set back from the course itself. A further golf course is planned, designed by Dave Thomas, with potential for several more in the years ahead. Created with care and understanding of the local environment on the edge of the Costa Vicentina nature reserve, Parque da Floresta is due to become a major player in the golfing expansion of the hitherto undersung western Algarve: a world apart, with a course to match.

REGIONAL DIRECTORY

Where to Stay

Lagos **Hotel de Lagos** (282 769967, Fax 282 769920) This well-established 4-star hotel is sited in the heart of Lagos. The relaxed, intimate ambience is deceptive, concealing the scale of the property, which has 304 bedrooms, 11 suites and is like a small village. Its interlinked buildings provide easy access to restaurants and other amenities and are cleverly designed, with multi-level walkways and terraces, to promote an informal atmosphere. There are three restaurants, plus another at the hotel's own beach club, A Duna. The hotel has outdoor and indoor swimming pools, the former heated in winter, the latter with jacuzzi, health club, hairdresser, shops and secure parking. The beach club also has a pool, tennis and watersports.

Armação de Pêra **Vila Vita Parc** (282 315310, Fax 282 315333) Within the context of a resort location based on discreet luxury, Vila Vita can probably satisfy the individual fantasies of all its guests. Designed over a sizeable area leading back from a dramatic clifftop and beach, the resort offers an imaginative world apart, with exotic gardens and water features, walkways winding through tropical trees and flowers, a multi-level swimming location at the Clubhouse overlooking the sea, a nine-hole pitch-and-putt golf course and a wide choice of accommodation, from designer hotel rooms to villas or apartments spread throughout the property, within which guests are transported by electric buggy. There are six restaurants, seven bars, a night club and a wine-tasting cellar. The main bar and lounge areas feel like a luxurious private home. Apart from the golf, with its teaching academy and full facilities, there is tennis, squash, volleyball, beach bathing, a yacht and watersports. The hotel has a hairdresser, beauty salon, health spa and shops.

Vilamoura **Dom Pedro Marina** (289 389802, Fax 289 313270) Located by the Vilamoura Marina complex, this warm, friendly 4-star hotel is popular with golfers. Its 100 rooms and 55 suites have views over the beach or marina, outdoor swimming pool and barbecue area. There is an indoor jacuzzi, spacious bar/lounge area and a restaurant which serves specialist Italian food and wine, as well as international cuisine. The hotel has a comprehensive shop and access to a wide range of sports facilities, including discounted golf rates.

Dom Pedro Golf (289 300700, Fax 289 300701) This is one of the original hotels in Vilamoura, long a favourite with golfers and now completely refurbished. Rated 4-star, there is a spacious bar and lounge area with live music in the evening, and a specialist golf reservation service. Apart from the airy restaurant, barbecues are a regular feature by the swimming pool in the tropical garden. There is a popular shop and a hairdresser.

Quinta do Lago **Hotel Quinta do Lago** (289 396666, Fax 289 396393) This luxury Orient Express hotel retains all the charm of its Portuguese character. Set deep within the verdant splendour of the Quinta do Lago estate, it has a fine hilltop sea view and lush gardens running down towards the Ria Formosa. Elegant but restrained, here service is a way of life and there are facilities to match. The Navegadores restaurant is noted for its lavish buffets and folk entertainment, the elegant Ca d'Oro for sumptuous à la carte and live music. There are heated indoor and outdoor swimming pools, health club, sauna, gymnasium and massage. The hotel is located within a cluster of four golf courses, with six more close by, and offers preferential rates. It also offers floodlit tennis, with watersports and riding nearby.

Portimão **Le Meridien – Penina Golf & Resort** (282 420200, Fax 282 420300) Centrepiece of a large estate with 36 holes of golf by Sir Henry Cotton, this imposing 5-star hotel has 196 rooms, restaurants, two outdoor swimming pools, tennis, riding, watersports, health centre, gymnasium, snooker, football pitch and shops.

Almancil **Le Meridien Dona Filipa** (289 394141, Fax 289 394288) Close to the beach on the Vale do Lobo estate, this elegant 5-star hotel has 147 rooms and delightful Portuguese decor. There are three restaurants, two bars, two outdoor heated pools and a health club. Meridien own the San Lorenzo golf course (15 minutes by courtesy bus) and there is also tennis, riding, cycle hire, watersports and deep-sea fishing.

Where to Eat

All the main hotels have good restaurants but one of the charms of the Algarve is the broad selection of small restaurants to be found all along the coast, offering typical Portuguese menus, fresh seafood, Italian, French, Chinese or Indian cuisine.

Ancora (282 69102), in Burgau, has fine food overlooking the sea. **A Eira do Mel** (282 66016), in Vila do Bispo, has an interesting, typically Portuguese menu, including wild boar, rabbit and fresh fish. **No Patio** (282 763777), in Lagos, includes Scandinavian and international dishes. **O Alberto** (282 769387), also in Lagos, is small, Algarvian and the proprietor cooks before you. **Dom Sebastião** (282 62795) is justifiably popular for traditional fare.

Grande Muralha (282 357380), in Carvoeiro, serves authentic Chinese with an Oriental smile. Also in Carvoeiro, **O Chefe Antonio** (282 358937) has an excellent reputation and a varied menu. **Hera** (282 312770), on the seafront at Armação de Pêra, offers friendly service and excellent fresh seafood. **Osteria Franco** (289 380849) in Vilamoura serves excellent Italian food in a rustic setting. **Casa Pituxa** (289 396238) and **La Brasserie des Amies** (289 399313), both in Almancil, provide popular dishes and excellent value. **Joe's Place** (289 392231), *en route* to Quinta do Lago, specializes in a variety of fresh fish while **Gigi** (0936 445178) on the Ria Formosa beach has a richly deserved reputation: reservation is essential. In Tavira, **Mares Restaurante** (281 81921) is best known for seafood *cataplana*.

What to See
Cabo de São Vicente is the most south-westerly point in Europe; in early history it marked the end of the then known world. A ruined fortress marks where Prince Henry the Navigator is said to have founded a navigation school around 1420, destroyed by Sir Francis

The approach shot view at the 9th hole on the Championship Course, Le Meridien-Penina Golf & Resort, with the hotel rising up behind.

Drake in 1587. There is an old church and a museum. The **Monchique Mountains** lie inland from Portimão, well-wooded and famous both for the production of charcoal and for the Caldas, a spa with reputedly healing waters. **Monchique** is a charming market town and centre for the local firewater, *medronho*. Stop off at the Olaria Pequena at **Porches** for highly collectable hand-crafted pottery.

Behind Carvoeiro lies **Silves**, a town with a rich history, a well-preserved castle, museum and cathedral. Towards Faro, visit **Loulé** just inland, famous for the 'Gypsy Market' on Saturdays and long traditions of craftsmanship in various metals as well as pottery, leather, candles and cane furniture. It also has some interesting churches including Nossa Senhora da Conceição with walls featuring scenes in blue and white *azulejos* (tiles). To the east, the pretty coastal town of **Tavira** is a fishing port with a colourful past, a historic bridge dating from Roman times and no less than 27 churches.

Portugal's Best 18 Holes

It seemed an interesting idea to create a dream course by selecting a sequence from all over Portugal. Each hole had to be correctly numbered and representative of its course, and only one hole was allowed from each. This is my personal selection: I have played them all and recommend them for their design quality and golfing pedigree. Play them yourself and see if you agree. Even if you don't, you will have played a third of Portugal's courses – arguably the best of them – and I hope you will have enjoyed them.

PORTUGAL'S BEST 18 HOLES

HOLE	YD	M	PAR	HOLE	YD	M	PAR
1	417	381	4	10	448	410	4
2	548	501	5	11	427	390	4
3	394	360	4	12	348	318	4
4	220	201	3	13	202	185	3
5	517	473	5	14	525	480	5
6	376	344	4	15	504	461	5
7	199	182	3	16	224	205	3
8	214	196	3	17	623	570	5
9	406	371	4	18	406	371	4
OUT	3291	3009	35	IN	3707	3390	37

6998YD • 6399M • PAR 72

Vila Sol
1st hole 417yd/381m par 4

A really tough opener, straight with just a touch of left turn near the green, the tilted fairway throws every shot left where strategic pines, including one guarding the green, come into play. A further cluster edges out from the right protecting, along with a large bunker, the elevated shelf of green.

Belas
2nd hole 548yds/501m par 5

From a high tee, the hole plunges down and right, a verdant funnel easing between impenetrable hillside and a large bunker

complex. A punitive creek moves in from the left to cross in front of the shallow green, also protected by sand and further scrub behind. A serious approach decision is required.

Vale da Pinta
3rd hole 394yd/360m par 4

Just short enough to reward the bold drive over the corner of the left-hand dogleg but with severe punishment for failure. Trees and bunkers cover the left half of the fairway, to catch anything underhit, while further trees, scrub and sand wait for the longer draw. There is open fairway right but this means a longer second to a tricky, elevated green.

2nd hole, Belas

3rd hole, Vale da Pinta

Santo da Serra
4th hole 220yd/201m par 3

This hole is both dramatic and demanding. From the tee, a sheer void drops away, leaving a shot that is all carry over space to a large shelf of green protected by one deep bunker in front and a shallow one behind. Beyond the green is sea; to the left, small houses deep in a valley 2100ft/640m below. It is the ultimate challenge across the 'top of the world' – with views to match.

Estoril
5th hole 517yd/473m par 5

A classic three-shotter on a much revered course. From tees cut into a hillside, the drive carries a lake through a narrow channel between encroaching trees. The fairway slopes severely left to right as well as uphill. Too far left and you are in the trees; a shade right and you kick into trees again. Hold your second left and yet more trees obstruct your approach to a steeply elevated two-tier green. Lightning-fast putts add to the challenge.

Palmares
6th hole 376yd/344m par 4

A fine example of biting off only what you can chew. The fairway doglegs gently right around a large area of wetland marsh, lush with sea grasses if not under water. The green, temptingly sited 276yd/251m away, dares the player to risk all or at least try to get close. Discretion is recommended; otherwise a lost ball is highly likely. Too far on a more cautious line will find trees or out-of-bounds by the railway. You have been warned.

Penha Longa
7th hole 199yd/182m par 3

A narrow short hole, with a large lake biting into the fairway all along the right–hand edge and further into the green, dominating your thoughts. A strategic bunker protects the front left corner and several mounds define the green. Play safe further left and your pitch may well skate across the slick putting surface into the water. Find the lake off the tee and your shot under penalty still faces much of the original challenge.

Ponte de Lima
8th hole 214yd/196m par 3

Apart from the spectacular view, a hole to give you nightmares. From an elevated tee, the green beckons temptingly below but a deep wooded ravine left with out-of-bounds is on the direct line. The putting surface is a slightly elevated plateau with no bunkers but steep slopes on three sides. (See page 97.)

4th hole, Santo da Serra

7th hole, Penha Longa

Pinheiros Altos
9th hole 406yd/371m par 4

A fine example of allowing nature to determine the strategic challenge of a hole. The natural slope of the land is to the left on this quite severe dogleg right, the green invisible from the tee. Trees and out-of-bounds protect the right; the downhill drive naturally runs left, risking further trees blocking the line to a well-bunkered, sloping, two-tier green. Careful placement, rather than length, is the key. (See page 23.)

Quinta do Lago
10th hole 448yd/410m par 4

Although the fairway looks broad and inviting off the tee, a single bunker left and encroaching trees and out-of-bounds right will punish anything drifting off line on this testing hole. The second shot has to carry a severe fairway valley to a large deep green with well-shaped bunkers on both sides. Careful club selection is crucial.

Vilamoura – The Old Course
11th hole 427yd/390m par 4

A fine golf hole with a sting in its tail. The downhill drive flatters to deceive, aiming to thread between two fairway bunkers and avoid the ranks of pine on this left-hand dogleg. The blind green lies well uphill, half-hidden behind a large bunker and trees on the right, as well as a steep fall-off. Precise club judgement and considerable skill is required to find the putting surface in two.

Quinta do Perú
12th hole 348yd/318m par 4

At first glance this may seem a piece of cake, but it needs to be handled with care. The large lake running up the left side poses the problems. Two clumps of trees and a single bunker narrow the fairway for the long hitter, while the water hazard eats in to absorb anything a touch left. Play safe and you face a longish second to a deep, narrow target with sand to the right, water front and left plus a slick, sloping putting surface.

Penina – Championship Course
13th hole 202yd/185m par 3

A great par 3, made more difficult by being dead flat. The direct route is all carry over water to a triangular green with mounds and a single bunker at the rear. The angled fairway allows shorter hitters to play safe, but beware a further mounded bunker to the left and out-of-bounds all along both sides of the hole. The left-to-right shape encourages courageous shots to drift right into the water hazard.

11th hole, Vilamoura Old Course

13th hole, Penina

Tróia
14th hole 525yd/480m par 5

A double-dogleg hole that makes the most of the typical terrain and hazards. The landing area for the drive is wide, but sandy scrub waits for any attempt to cut the corner. The hole narrows as the fairway turns left past pines, then eases along a vast waste bunker right which, with a couple of smaller sand traps left, protects the narrow, angled, slightly elevated green, backed by bushes and sand.

Aroeira 1
15th hole 504yd/461m par 5

Another double-dogleg of considerable guile and subtlety. The drive is uphill, with tall pines edging out from the right in the landing area on the crest. The ideal second needs to be held right on a down-sloping fairway tilted left. Play too far left, and trees bordering the left-hand lake hamper your approach to the narrow green. Play safely right and your third must carry a large bunker and hold the shallow target before reaching the water.

Vale do Lobo – Royal Course
16th hole 224yd/205m par 3

On what is probably the most famous hole in Portugal, the direct route involves a dramatic carry over yawning chasms of jagged ochre cliff and a large bunker in front of the shallow green: a long shot, never mind the spectacular sea view. A more cautious approach can find a sliver of fairway on the right to leave, with luck, a pitch and putt. (See page 31.)

Praia d'El Rey
17th hole 623yd/570m par 5

The challenge here is based on factors that typify the course – sandy dunes and scrub lining every fairway and an ever-present sea breeze. There are no bunkers except one behind the green, but there is plenty of trouble on this gently rising dogleg left. The landing areas narrow severely for the long drive and second shot, towards a well-elevated, narrow green fronting a vast dune.

San Lorenzo
18th hole 406 yd/371m par 4

A worthy finishing hole for the dream course. The tee shot, to a snaking fairway tilted right to left, needs to hug the left edge to shorten the demanding second shot, but risks a large lake running all along the hole. Play safer right and one strategic bunker looms; the approach will also need more club. The shot has to carry the lake fronting the shallow green, bunkered front and back with no real bail-out alternative. (See page 25.)

14th hole, Tróia

15th hole, Aroeira 1

Chapter 2

Lisbon and Surrounds

It may come as some surprise to golfing visitors to discover that the Lisbon region, encompassing diverse areas within an hour's drive of the capital city, can offer nearly as much golf, and certainly as many courses of genuinely high quality, as the better-known Algarve coast to the south. By comparison, courses here are less crowded, green fees are lower and, most important, all of the sophisticated charms and pleasures of one of the world's most elegant cities are close at hand.

Improved motorway networks, a second bridge south over the Tagus River and an international airport within ten minutes' drive of the city centre, provide unrivalled access both to Lisbon itself and to the good selection of golfing locations nearby. The seaside `spa town of Estoril and its near neighbour Cascais form the hub of golfing activity to

Left: Medieval cobbled streets typify the walled town of Obidos. Above: The 16th-century Tower of Belem in Lisbon provided protection against naval invaders.

the west, an elegant environment long favoured by European royalty and those with wealth or the right connections. With its grand hotels, palatial casino and established place in Portuguese history, Estoril has an ageless attraction and much to offer the visitor.

Across the river to the south, the Costa Azul charms by contrast. A region of rolling pinewoods, vineyards and coastal fishing villages, it encompasses the busy estuary of the Sado River, the pine-encrusted slopes of the Serra da Arrábida – a strikingly beautiful natural park spilling down into the sea – and a host of historic castles and other landmarks testifying to Portugal's past.

To the north, golf is establishing a determined foothold in the area around the medieval walled town of Obidos, where a wealth of untouched sandy shoreline and forested heath is available. All the locations are easily reached from Lisbon; all offer varied delights, and much more than golf alone.

LISBON AND SURROUNDS

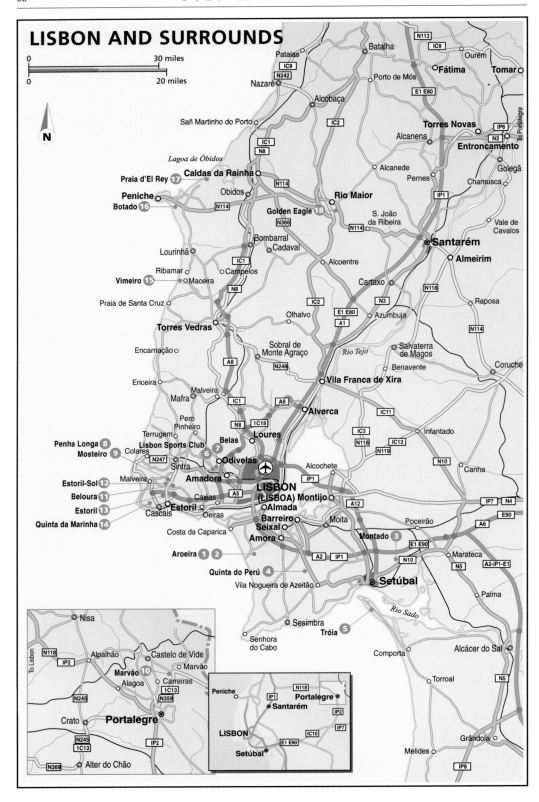

0   30 miles

0   20 miles

N

Pataias
Batalha
Ourém
Fátima
Tomar
Porto de Mós
Nazaré
Alcobaça
Saň Martinho do Porto
Torres Novas
Alcanena
Entroncamento
Golegã
Alcanede
Pernes
Chamusca
Lagoa de Óbidos
Praia d'El Rey **17** Caldas da Rainha
Rio Maior
Peniche
Obidos
Botado **16**
Golden Eagle **18**
S. João da Ribeira
Santarém
Almeirim
Lourinhã
Bombarral
Cadaval
Ribamar
Campélos
Alcoentre
Vale de Cavalos
Vimeiro **15** Maceira
Cartaxo
Raposa
Praia de Santa Cruz
Olhalvo
Azumbuja
Torres Vedras
Sobral de Monte Agraço
Rio Tejo
Salvaterra de Magos
Coruche
Encarnação
Benavente
Ericeira
Mafra
Malveira
Vila Franca de Xira
Pero Pinheiro
Alverca
Terrugem
Belas
Loures
Infantado
Penha Longa **8**
Lisbon Sports Club **7**
Mosteiro **9** Colares
Odivelas
Canha
Sintra
Amadora
Alcochete
LISBON (LISBOA) Montijo
Estoril-Sol **12**
Malveira
Caxias
Almada
Beloura **11**
Estoril **13**
Cascais
Barreiro
Poceirão
Quinta da Marinha **14**
Oeiras
Moita
Montado **3**
Costa da Caparica
Seixal
Amora
Aroeira **1 2**
Setúbal
Quinta do Perú **4**
MaU reca
Vila Nogueira de Azeitão
Palma
Sesimbra
Tróia **5**
Rio Sado
Senhora do Cabo
Comporta
Alcácer do Sal
Torroal
Grândola
Melides

Nisa
To Lisbon
Alpalhão
Castelo de Vide
Marvão
Marvão **10**
Alagoa
Carreiras
Crato
Portalegre
Alter do Chão

Peniche
Portalegre
Santarém
LISBON
Setúbal

Traditional culture is most evident in the wealth of fairs and festivals, saints' days and carnivals occuring all year in towns and villages throughout the region. Here, costumes, music and dances handed down over centuries reflect the area's rich history and the many influences that have made it such a fascinating tourist destination. Religion, the sea and the rich diversity of local handicrafts and cuisine all play a part.

Shopping for products made by the local craftspeople is a genuine adventure. From delicate filigree jewellery in gold or silver to traditional wooden furniture or basketwork, each offers its specialities. Look for leather goods, fine copper work, embroidery, tapestry and lace as well as hand-crafted pottery and ceramics, including a wealth of hand-painted decorative tiles (*azulejos*), a Portuguese speciality.

Good food and wine are an essential part of life, whether enjoyed in one of the luxury restaurants just off the Avenida da Liberdade or on the heights of Alfama or the Bairro Alto, where the mournful strains of *fado* could not be more typical. For really fresh fish and seafood, the fishing villages of Cascais and Sesimbra are hard to beat. Try barbecued sardines and mackerel, clams steamed with pork or sea bass cooked in a salt crust. Languostine, live crab and lobster may be on offer: check the price. The choice of delicate sweets and hand-made cheeses is legion; leave room for the custard tarts, a local speciality.

A romantic 19th-century restoration of a ruined monastery, the Pena Palace towers on a mountain-top overlooking the historic town of Sintra.

SAUDADE: THE SOUL OF FADO

From obscure origins, *fado* developed in the sailors' taverns of Lisbon in the early 19th century. Summed up in the word *saudade*, its haunting, heartbreaking melodies, sung with great emotion, reveal a longing for the past in songs of lost love, broken dreams and cruel fate, with an expression of feeling that is much more than mere entertainment. *Fado* taverns, located mainly in the Alfama and Bairro Alto districts, are popular with locals as well as visitors. In a sombre, candlelit atmosphere, the singer is accompanied by two guitarists, one with a classical instrument, the other with a heart-shaped 12-string guitar played with a plectrum. The greatest performer of *fado* is the internationally renowned Amalia Rodriguez.

Aroeira 1

Clube de Campo de Portugal, Herdade da Aroeira,
Fonte da Telha, 2815-207 Charneca da Caparica
TEL: *(21) 297 1345* **FAX:** *(21) 297 1238*
LOCATION: *10 miles/16km south of Lisbon, off N377*
COURSE: *18 holes, 6605yd/6040m, par 72, SSS 72*
TYPE OF COURSE: *Winding, gently undulating course carved from a mature pine forest*
DESIGNER: *Frank Pennink (1972)*
GREEN FEES: *EE*
FACILITIES: *Pro shop, cart, trolley and equipment hire, driving range, chipping practice area with bunker, putting greens, bar and restaurant in clubhouse*
VISITORS: *Welcome with handicap certificate; soft spikes only*

AROEIRA							
HOLE	YD	M	PAR	HOLE	YD	M	PAR
1	531	485	5	10	527	482	5
2	435	398	4	11	396	362	4
3	418	382	4	12	377	345	4
4	177	162	3	13	377	345	4
5	387	354	4	14	140	128	3
6	349	319	4	15	504	461	5
7	411	376	4	16	158	144	3
8	208	190	3	17	332	304	4
9	507	464	5	18	371	339	4
OUT	3423	3130	36	IN	3182	2910	36

6605YD • 6040M • PAR 72

Despite its proximity to Lisbon, the Costa Azul has managed to exist in relative tourist obscurity even though it has several of the best golf courses in Portugal. Longest-established but still enjoying a high reputation, Aroeira is a reclusive gem of genuine class. When the course was opened in 1972, it was tucked away peacefully in the centre of a large pine forest. Since then, many luxury properties have been erected around it but have not disturbed the essential charm of the course, which has matured into a major championship venue. The estate now has a large swimming complex, a further 18 holes by

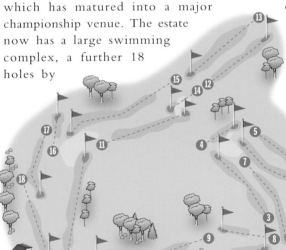

Donald Steel opened in summer 2000 (see page 62) and plans for a golf teaching school, an equestrian centre and a central hotel/clubhouse.

Aroeira is another example of the legacy of Frank Pennink, English-born creator of the Old Course at Vilamoura and Palmares in the Algarve, whose talent and concept of letting nature dictate course strategy wherever possible has stood the test of time. The holes wind through tall avenues of pine, with lush Bermuda fairways enlivened by birdsong and a colourful carpet of wild flowers. Each hole presents a different challenge; each is separate from the rest and all are notable for the complete absence of fairway bunkers. It is easy to remove trees to form a golf course; Pennink's skill lay in knowing which to leave, and it is these which ordain play, rendering additional hazards unnecessary.

Although it plays reasonably long, the course is as much a test of placement off the tee. The fairways, many doglegged, are deceptively wide but require a well-positioned shot to open up the approach to the green. It is all too easy to find the short grass yet have an errant branch blocking the line to the flag. Aroeira is a course of considerable subtlety,

only apparent on renewed acquaintance. Its pedigree was recognized with the staging of the Portuguese Open here from 1996 to 1999.

Part of the appeal of the course is its sense of forested seclusion. Though only a short distance from the capital city, it is worlds away in its green harmony with nature. The single-storey clubhouse follows this theme, its rustic timbered charm blending happily with its wholly natural surroundings.

Like most good courses, Aroeira's back nine demands respect, and two holes are more than reminiscent of Augusta's 'Amen Corner'. The lookalike 11th, 396yd/362m from the back, needs a long uphill drive to make the challenging approach visible. The small green is

The approach shot view down to the semi-island green of the 396yd/362m par-4 11th, a small, demanding target in a most picturesque setting.

downhill, well defended by water and sand, with little room for error. Precision is also needed at the 14th, a dead ringer for Augusta's par-3 12th: only 140yd/128m across water, open to fickle crosswinds and with sand to front and rear, it is a cute card-wrecker.

The double-dogleg 15th follows, demanding careful placement to avoid impeding trees and reach a downhill, well-bunkered green bordered by water – another fine hole in this demanding yet extremely beautiful test of the game. (See page 55.)

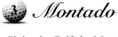 Aroeira 2

Clube de Campo de Portugal, Herdade da Aroeira,
Fonte da Telha, 2815-207 Charneca da Caparica
TEL: *(21) 297 1345* **FAX:** *(21) 297 1238*
LOCATION: *See Aroeira 1, page 60*
COURSE: *18 holes, 6685yd/6113m, par 72, SSS 72*
TYPE OF COURSE: *Winding, gently undulating course
through mature pine forest with lakes*
DESIGNER: *Donald Steel (2000)*
GREEN FEES: *EE weekdays; EEE weekends*
FACILITIES: *Pro shop, cart, trolley and equipment
hire, driving range, putting green, bar and restaurant*
VISITORS: *Handicap certificate required; soft
spikes only*

Opened in April 2000, the second course at Aroeira has been laid out through an adjacent location of similar, gently undulating woodland by Donald Steel. With sympathetic understanding of the natural design philosophy of his mentor Frank Pennink, previously shown at Vila Sol in the Algarve, Steel has made good use of the land, adding additional water features in open areas.

Tall pine trees are a key feature on every hole of this new course, lining fairly straight but often tight fairways leading to small, well-shaped, elevated greens with deep bunkering. Water hazards eat strategically into the landing area of a number of holes, most notably at the 9th, a 405yd/370m par 4. Rated toughest on the scorecard, the drive is played from a series of tree-flanked raised tees across a large lake which runs along most of the right-hand side of the narrow dogleg fairway. Placement is crucial at this testing hole, with the approach uphill to a tilted green framed with pines.

 Montado

Clube de Golf do Montado, Apartado 40, Algeruz,
2950 Palmela
TEL: *(265) 706648* **FAX:** *(265) 706775*
LOCATION: *3 miles/5km north-east of Setúbal on N10*
COURSE: *18 holes, 6567yd/6003m, par 72, SSS 72*
TYPE OF COURSE: *Relatively open, gently sloping land
with some cork and other trees*
DESIGNER: *Duarte Sottomayor (1992)*
GREEN FEES: *EE*
FACILITIES: *Pro shop, cart, trolley and equipment hire,
tuition, driving range, pitching and putting greens,
changing facilities, bar and restaurant in clubhouse*
VISITORS: *Welcome*

Montado offers an undemanding alternative to the championship challenges of the Costa Azul. Its broad fairways, gentle slopes and large greens are popular with newer golfers and those playing off high handicaps. Another effort by Duarte Sottomayor, designer of Estela in the north, it incorporates many of the same features. The majority of the greens are elevated, with bunkers on either side of the approach.

The best hole on an unimaginative layout is the par-3 8th, 184yd/168m to an elevated two-level green, ringed by trees behind and deep bunkers in front, which requires bravery and finesse in equal measure. The site offers the attractive opportunity to play past working vineyards (with the club's own-label wine on hand at the 19th) and some ancient cork oaks, backed by a forest of mature trees and views of distant hills. The large split-level clubhouse, although lacking atmosphere, offers adequate facilities.

*The 5th hole at Montado, a tight uphill dogleg left, is well
protected by cork oaks, sand and water.*

Resort Golf: a Growth Industry

It took nearly 50 years (from 1890) before there were six golf courses in Portugal; another 30 to double the number. In the next 30 years, up to 1999, the number mushroomed to a national total nudging 50, and the pace is accelerating. It is estimated that there will be 100 courses open throughout the country within the next five years.

Of projects currently under construction or planned, the Algarve has the lion's share. Castro Marim Golf & Country Club, near the border with Spain, is due to open 18 holes during the year 2000, with a further 18 holes by 2002. Vilamoura's new Millennium Course was inaugurated in May 2000, in addition to the recently launched Butch Harmon Teaching Academy. A further Vilamoura course, by Arnold Palmer, will follow. Other projects include 18 holes at Espiche near Lagos; 18 holes at Parque de Floresta by Dave Thomas, plus a further 18; courses at Pinheiros Altos, Morgado do Reguengo at Portimão; Quinta da Boavista near Lagos; Quinta da Laranja near Silves; São Braz at Quinta do Lago and Vila Nova de Cacela near Tavira. Nine-hole projects include the Balaia Village near Albufeira and a further loop at Vila Sol.

The Costa Azul expects a further nine holes at Quinta do Perú and a new course near Tróia. Lisbon has 18 holes planned at Cabanas

Some of the new holes of Vilamoura's Millennium Course wind through a dense forest of umbrella pine, typical of the undulating, sandy terrain so ideal for golf.

plus nine at Bela Vista. The Quinta da Marinha estate, beyond Cascais, is currently completing the 18 holes of Oitavos Golfe to double its golfing capacity. A little further north, Obidos and Figuera de Foz each have 18 holes planned.

This swelling tide of course construction is matched by concerns about environmental damage from over-development, chemical treatments and natural habitat destruction. The prime example is Vilamoura, the largest golf resort in Portugal, where the award-winning and far-sighted Vilamoura XXI programme is already in its second phase, covering an area in excess of 2,000 acres/810ha. It is planned as a green town, with 30,000 permanent residents by 2010. Preserving the environment is a top priority, implementing 'green' policies for tree planting, waste and land management and water reclamation. Areas of natural wetland have been set aside for wildlife conservation.

Several Algarve courses border the Ria Formosa, the 37 mile/60km lagoon system along the coast that is a protected area of special interest and home to a wide variety of bird, sea and plant life. Other courses linked to protected conservation areas are Parque da Floresta, Belas Clube de Campo and Quinta da Marinha, where the new Oitavos location is part of the Audubon International ecological programme.

Quinta do Perú

Clube Quinta do Perú, 2830 Quinta do Conde
TEL: *(21) 213 4320* **FAX:** *(21) 213 4321*
E-MAIL: *golf@quinta-do-peru.com*
LOCATION: *6 miles / 10km west of Setúbal on N10 at Azeitão*
COURSE: *18 holes, 6601yd / 6036m, par 72, SSS 72*
TYPE OF COURSE: *Elevated, gently sloped sandy land with mature pine trees; large areas of strategic sand and water*
DESIGNER: *Rocky Roquemore (1994)*
GREEN FEES: *EEE*
FACILITIES: *Pro shop, cart, trolley and equipment hire, tuition, driving range, putting green, changing facilities, bar and restaurant*
VISITORS: *Welcome; maximum handicap: men 28, ladies 36*

QUINTA DO PERÚ

HOLE	YD	M	PAR	HOLE	YD	M	PAR
1	563	515	5	10	526	481	5
2	372	340	4	11	172	157	3
3	195	178	3	12	348	318	4
4	383	350	4	13	491	449	5
5	538	492	5	14	332	304	4
6	338	309	4	15	389	356	4
7	366	335	4	16	195	178	3
8	218	199	3	17	352	322	4
9	400	366	4	18	423	387	4
OUT	3373	3084	36	IN	3228	2952	36

6601YD • 6036M • PAR 72

The owners of Quinta do Perú, Portugal's largest banking family, have shown considerable restraint in the allocation of land for the golf course. Set amongst endless tracts of virgin pine forest, the beautifully crafted course actually looks down on the rest of the property (and much of the housing development) – a rare arrangement indeed. The holes afford superb views over the treetops to distant hills and the ancient fortress of Palmela. Favoured with sandy soil and well-established pines, American designer Rocky Roquemore was able to create a fine course over the gently undulating plateau and its surrounding slopes. The course is a pleasure to play from the normal tees; a genuine test from the back.

This is a course with class, making excellent use of the natural land to give an essentially Portuguese flavour despite large penal areas of American-style sand and water. The succession of holes offers considerable variety, flowing past open spaces, through narrowing stands of tall pines and curving seductively around the adjacent hillside. Yet, at the same time, it maintains a strand of continuity and style that underlines the restraint of the architect in allowing the trees and terrain largely to dictate play.

There is much to admire and enjoy at Quinta do Perú. Every golf club has a personality, a presence, which colours your perception and appreciation of its virtues. At Perú, relaxation is the key. There is a sense of space, of well-organized, unhurried permanence, that belies the club's very short history. From the delightfully understated rustic timber clubhouse to the casual elegance of the course, you can feel instantly at home rather than a visitor. The greens, always in prime condition, are deceptively sloped and faster than they appear.

Above: Putting out on the 9th with a majestic view across to the Palmela Hills. Below: The 15th green is well protected by sand and water.

Four holes illustrate the subtle, strategic demands of the course. The par-5 13th, 491yd/449m from the championship markers, requires a drive from an elevated tee to a narrow landing area embraced by pines and sand. Play straight but safe, and an angled creek challenges your second on a hole doglegging left. Carry it, and a copse on the corner blocks many approaches to an uphill, well-defended green. Two holes later, the 389yd/356m 15th appears a pushover, but the downhill fairway is tightly trapped and the approach flirts with a large lake nudging up to a narrow green.

Two other holes, both par 3s, stand out. The 8th is 218yd/199m from the back tee, and all carry over water to a relatively shallow target with sand at the back. The 16th is similar, demanding a 195yd/178m shot over water to a steeply sloping angled green bunkered to the right and rear.

Laid out in a delightfully natural setting and kept in immaculate condition, Quinta do Perú is both a pleasure to play and a test. It has already deservedly hosted the final event of the European Challenge Tour. In the clubhouse, the menu and wine list are worth examination, providing a fitting finale to a scenic and memorable round of golf.

Tróia

*Tróia Golf, Complexo Turistico de Tróia, 7570
Grândola*
TEL: *(265) 499335* **FAX:** *(265) 494315*
LOCATION: *10 miles/17km south of Setúbal (via car
ferry) on N253-1*
COURSE: *18 holes, 6930yd/6337m, par 72, SSS 74*
TYPE OF COURSE: *Pine-lined, gently undulating course
laid out over a sandy promontory by the sea*
DESIGNER: *Robert Trent Jones (1980)*
GREEN FEES: *EE*
FACILITIES: *Golf shop, cart, trolley and equipment hire,
driving range, pitching and putting greens, changing
facilities, swimming pool, bar and restaurant in clubhouse*
VISITORS: *Welcome*

HOLE	YD	M	PAR	HOLE	YD	M	PAR
1	515	471	5	10	341	312	4
2	209	191	3	11	176	161	3
3	405	370	4	12	376	344	4
4	156	143	3	13	455	416	4
5	435	398	4	14	525	480	5
6	448	410	4	15	441	403	4
7	545	498	5	16	443	405	4
8	337	308	4	17	174	159	3
9	412	377	4	18	537	491	5
OUT	3463	3166	36	IN	3468	3171	36

TRÓIA

6931YD • 6337M • PAR 72

Robert Trent Jones, whose golfing gems span the globe, found an ideal location on the narrow sandbar of Tróia, a 20-minute ferry trip across the Sado estuary from Setúbal. The gently undulating sandy land bordering the sea, encrusted with established pine and native flora and cooled by the sea breeze, was a gift to a creative golf architect. The result is a masterpiece, a combination of nature and strategy that is generally reckoned to be the toughest 18 holes in Portugal.

In a way, the slightly inaccessible location has only added to Tróia's reputation and mystique. This was underlined when the Portuguese Open was played here in 1982, and the winner, Sam Torrance, was the only player in the field to finish under par. Relatively narrow driving lines down dogleg ranks of pine demand accuracy to narrow slivers of fairway. The problems are compounded by the rough – or rather, the lack of it. Miss the fairway at Tróia and you will find yourself in unraked natural waste sand and scrub under trees. Finding the fairway is only half the battle, however. Small greens, well-protected by deep bunkers, demand high well-struck approach shots. There are no easy pars here, only a succession of varied challenges, each tempered by the coastal seascape, with views of the Arrábida mountains and an omnipresent breeze.

Originally laid out nearly 20 years ago, the course has suffered minor changes and has sometimes failed to show itself in prime condition in recent years. Now, new investment heralds a rebirth of the entire Tróia development. Many changes to the surrounding infrastructure are planned and efforts are in hand to bring the course back to its original condition and quality. One of Europe's finest golfing challenges is also planned to be one of its best maintained, without of course compromising its essentially rugged nature.

Every hole poses a special problem at Tróia; each is a very individual examination of a golfer's abilities over essentially natural terrain. One of the great gifts possessed by Trent Jones, despite hailing from a country where the majority of courses tend to be artificial, is his ability to recognize where the hand of nature can be left well alone and creative restraint is a virtue. Troia is an excellent example.

Two holes can serve to summarize its challenges, always open to a fickle offshore breeze. The shortest is the 4th, 156yd/143m from the back tee and nudging the beach. It is the second short hole in the first four and a potential card-wrecker. The steeply elevated green narrows towards the rear, with waste sand and out-of-bounds to the left and a cavernous bunker to the right. Miss either side and you have a genuine problem. Also in the front nine is the par-5 7th, at 545yd/498m the longest hole on the course. The dramatic double-dogleg right is

The tee of the 443yd/405m par-4 16th is typical of the landscape at Tróia, a green ribbon threading narrowly past pines, scrub and rolling sand dunes.

ROBERT TRENT JONES

Although golf courses have existed for over 300 years, the recognition of course designers dates only from the late 19th century. The first to study as a professional golf architect (by taking courses in engineering, agronomy and landscape architecture), and undoubtedly the most influential figure of the last 70 years, is Robert Trent Jones. Born in England in 1906, he moved to the USA as a child and became a scratch player, but gave up serious competition owing to illness. Over 400 courses in 28 countries worldwide testify to his skill and appeal, and many have been chosen for major events. His dramatic layouts are notable for 'heroic' design, with large strategic areas of sand and water, following his philosophy of 'easy bogey, difficult par'. His sons, Robert Jr and Rees, also have international reputations in course design.

compounded by a narrowing fairway and a severe kink partway, with strategic trees, two sand traps and water edging in from the left. Accurate placement and length are vital to set up the approach to a small, shallow, heavily bunkered green. With waste sand and scrub waiting to catch you on either side, a bogey here is quite acceptable.

Early Golf – British Links

The history of golf in Portugal is, in many respects, more British than Portuguese. The British introduced the game to the country in the 19th century and for the first 40 years were almost the only players. In the golfing boom that began in the 1960s they have been the prime innovators and developers, and have formed the major part of the holiday market.

Golf in Portugal began at Espinho, an area of sandy coastal linksland just south of Oporto in the north. A group of British wine exporters who missed their native pursuits formed the Oporto Niblicks Club in 1890. Nine holes were laid out near the railway, essential for access in those pre-motoring days. One hole was even played across the Lisbon–Oporto line, a feat apparently only attempted after suitable fortification with a glass of port.

Renamed the Oporto Golf Club in 1901, it remained an exclusive preserve of the British community for the next 30 years. The first president was Charles Neville Skeffington, whose widow presented the club with the Skeffington Cup, the world's oldest club trophy to remain in continuous competition.

Portuguese involvement in the game developed slowly, possibly due to insular British resistance, and the first national member appeared only in 1920. It was 1931 before a Portuguese player won a club

The Skeffington Cup – played for annually over 18 holes of medal play since J.D. Smart won in 1891.

competition and, at the last count, there were still only 12,000 registered domestic players in the country. The nine holes at Oporto remained until 1934, when the course was expanded to become the first 18-hole layout in Portugal.

Next on the scene was the Lisbon Sports Club, formed to serve the sporting interests of British telephone and railway company employees. Along with football, cricket and tennis, its members played golf from 1900, eventually forming a golf club in 1922. Hard on its heels came Estoril on the Costa Lisboa in 1928, while nine holes were created at Miramar in 1932 as a means of allowing more Portuguese to play the game. Marking its popularity as a holiday retreat for Oporto's elite, Vidago's nine holes were opened in 1936. Even such outposts as Madeira and the Azores were not immune, as the British residents created Santo da Serra on the former in 1936 while a far-sighted Portuguese commissioned Furnas in 1939.

Seven courses were in play, heavily patronized by British residents, by the beginning of World War II. Even in 1970, when package tourism was starting to flower, there were only 12 courses in the country. Now there are over 50, with more under construction, and the Portuguese game has clearly come a long way since the early efforts of the Oporto Niblicks.

6 Lisbon Sports Club

Lisbon Sports Club, Casal de Carregueira, 2745 Belas
TEL: *(21) 431 0077/432 1474* **FAX:** *(21) 431 2482*
LOCATION: *7 miles/11km north-west of Lisbon off N117*
COURSE: *18 holes, 5774yd/5280m, par 69, SSS 69*
TYPE OF COURSE: *Parkland, with many holes curving around low wooded hills and crossed by a strategic stream; plenty of mature trees*
DESIGNERS: *Hawtree & Sons; Fernando Nunes Pedro (1962/1992)*
GREEN FEES: *EE*
FACILITIES: *Golf shop, cart, trolley and equipment hire, tuition, caddies, changing facilities, bar, restaurant, tennis, sauna, swimming pool*
VISITORS: *Welcome weekdays with handicap certificate*

For most people, golf in Portugal is inextricably linked with the sun-soaked Algarve and the holiday courses which have sprung up in recent years. However, this club was well established around 1880 and had a six-hole course near Alges from 1900.

Originally set up as a sporting club by British expatriate employees of the Eastern Telegraph Company to indulge their passions for cricket, football and tennis, the golf club recently celebrated its 75th anniversary after moving from Carcavelos and Aguila to its present site in 1962. Originally nine holes created by the British firm of Hawtree & Sons, the course now offers a full 18 holes on the same site. No doubt the early sporting pioneers had quite a trek out of Lisbon to the club, but new motorway links provide ready access to a piece of Portugal's golfing history.

The clubhouse, set up on the hillside overlooking the course, was the original house of the property, an elegant mansion full of reminders of the club's history, with a fine restaurant and relaxed balcony views of some of the holes and the surrounding wooded hills. Play on the lower holes is governed by a winding stream and many mature eucalyptus trees. A steep hill provides further interest on a shortish, essentially private members' course where you will, however, be made welcome.

The view down the tilting fairway of the par-4 9th, where pines and eucalyptus wait to gather your ball.

Belas

Belas Clube de Campo, Alameda do Aqueduto, 2745 Belas
TEL: *(21) 962 6130* **FAX:** *(21) 962 6131*
E-MAIL: *belas.golfe@mail.telepac.pt*
LOCATION: *7 miles/11km north-west of Lisbon off N117*
COURSE: *18 holes, 6977yd/6380m, par 72, SSS 72*
TYPE OF COURSE: *Open rolling slopes along hillsides and valleys with large areas of sand and water*
DESIGNER: *Rocky Roquemore (1997)*
GREEN FEES: *EEE*
FACILITIES: *Pro shop, cart, trolley and equipment hire, tuition, driving range, chipping and putting greens, changing facilities, bar, restaurant*
VISITORS: *Welcome*

HOLE	YD	M	PAR	HOLE	YD	M	PAR
1	419	383	4	10	542	496	5
2	548	501	5	11	391	358	4
3	448	410	4	12	407	372	4
4	383	350	4	13	380	347	4
5	224	205	3	14	196	179	3
6	553	506	5	15	498	455	5
7	213	195	3	16	352	322	4
8	350	320	4	17	164	150	3
9	462	422	4	18	447	409	4
OUT	3600	3292	36	IN	3377	3088	36

BELAS

6977YD • 6380M • PAR 72

The game has come full circle near the small town of Belas, on the north-western fringe of Lisbon. Sited literally across the road from its historic, well-established neighbour, the Lisbon Sports Club, the new residential community of Belas Clube de Campo can boast a course built to the most modern specifications, with infrastructure to match. The contrast could not be more complete.

Carved through valleys and over the rolling slopes of Carregueira, an area of fairly inhospitable hills, Belas was something of a *tour de force* for American designer Rocky Roquemore. The rugged hillsides, with sparse vegetation, only accentuate the lush green succession of gently mounded fairways, large scalloped bunkers and areas of penal water. To build a golf course here was an achievement in itself; to produce one in such superb condition, nestling comfortably within the succession of rolling hills, is a triumph.

The architect has seized the opportunity to create golf of genuinely high quality, using a broad brush. The velvet fairways, winding greenly past seductive areas of sand and – in the closing holes – water, are a delight. As the course progresses, the challenge mounts, with changing elevation affecting club selection.

The houses on the hills above may make you feel under surveillance at times but the quality of the golf will keep you entranced and involved.

The front nine flows through dramatic, naturally preserved slopes in splendid isolation, whereas the back nine follows more open country within the

development rim. One of the most memorable holes comes early, the 548yd/501m par-5 2nd, called 'Augusta' (see page 52). In some respects, it offers a mirror-image of the 13th hole at the Masters and a similar challenge. From an elevated tee, the hole plunges down and right, a verdant funnel easing past rugged slopes and bunkers to reach a shallow green fronted by a punitive creek, prompting a serious approach decision.

The project is one of a number of major developments by the André Jordan group, which include the Vilamoura complex in the Algarve. Considerable building work is already in progress on the higher ground, where individual homes and clusters of apartments have views down over the two-year-old course and away to Sintra in the west. This satellite residential development so near to Lisbon has good access to the new motorway network and forms part of a master-planned community project to integrate housing across the hills with golf in the valleys, sheltered from the prevailing

Above: A glorious view from the 12th tee, curving right past tall trees and sand. Below: The long and narrow 18th threads between large bunkers and water.

winds. Over 1,000 trees, mainly pines, will enrich the landscape over time. The attractive clubhouse, pleasantly sited above the final green, offers panoramic views over several holes and a tastefully designed restaurant.

8 Penha Longa

*Caesar Park Penha Longa, Estrada de Lagoa Azul,
Linhó, 2710 Sintra*
TEL: *(21) 924 9011* **FAX:** *(21) 924 9024*
LOCATION: *3 miles/5km north-west of Estoril on N9
at Lagoa Azul*
COURSE: *Atlantico: 18 holes, 6881yd/6290m, par
72, SSS 73; see also next entry, page 74*
TYPE OF COURSE: *Laid out over mountain foothills,
often seriously sloped, some wooded holes, some open*
DESIGNER: *Robert Trent Jones Jr (1992)*
GREEN FEES:*EEEE*
FACILITIES: *Pro shop, cart, trolley, equipment and shoe
hire, golf academy tuition, driving range, driving and
chipping greens with bunkers, halfway house, tennis,
swimming pool, changing facilities, bar and restaurant in
clubhouse*
VISITORS: *Welcome; handicap certificate required (no
jeans)*

				PENHA LONGA ATLANTICO COURSE			
HOLE	YD	M	PAR	HOLE	YD	M	PAR
1	366	335	4	10	418	382	4
2	396	362	4	11	393	359	4
3	354	324	4	12	495	453	5
4	434	397	4	13	352	322	4
5	209	191	3	14	417	381	4
6	498	455	5	15	197	180	3
7	199	182	3	16	440	402	4
8	556	508	5	17	204	187	3
9	409	374	4	18	542	496	5
OUT	3421	3128	36	IN	3458	3162	36

6879YD • 6290M • PAR 72

A visit to Penha Longa is not only about golf, it is also a date with history. It is arguably one of the finest golfing resort developments in the country, benefiting from the happy combination of an outstanding site, imaginative design and considerable investment.

The course has been built around a grand palace and church which was founded in the 14th century as a Hieronymite monastery and later became the summer retreat of Portuguese royalty. Ancient gardens and water features, dating from the 15th and 16th centuries, remain to enhance the protected environment of the estate.

The main course was carefully sculpted into the foothills of the Sintra mountains by Robert Trent Jones Jr, and opened in 1992. A course of genuine quality, it lives up to the American architect's philosophy of creating courses that are manageable from the members' tees but pose a considerably tougher test from the back. The terrain, heavily wooded in parts, elevated and open to prevailing winds in others, proved a challenge to the designer's skill. Steep gradients provide some testing holes and, from the higher ground, spectacular views towards the sea.

The project is a triumph for the Aoki Corporation, a multinational conglomerate with a sincere commitment to preserving the protected environment and its proliferation of natural vegetation and wildlife. Housing development has been located in limited, relatively unobtrusive areas, and the on-site hotel, Caesar Park, blends happily into the wooded setting, its pastel tones and classic lines in harmony with its historic neighbour. In contrast, the hotel interior offers palatial splendour and oceans of marble.

Playing Penha Longa provides many memories. Most visitors will recall how they handled the 6th and 7th holes. The former has an ancient stone aqueduct and water-tower bordering its green; the latter (see page 53) is a truly challenging 199yd/182m par 3 protected by sand left and water all along the right.

Like all good designs, the course saves its real examination for the closing holes. The 15th, a beautiful par 3 of 197yd/180m across water to a green backed by mountains, demands accuracy with mounds, sand and a severe down-slope punishing less than perfect shots (see page 11). The 16th, at 440yd/402m par 4, rated stroke 1, is memorable. Off a high tee, the drive must find a mounded, undulating fairway, avoiding three bunkers at the corner of the right-hand dogleg. From here, the hole bends steeply uphill to a kidney-shaped plateau green, where only a high carry will hold.

After that, the short 17th, 204yd/187m but sharply downhill through trees, may seem a relief. But two bunkers and severe side-slopes punish anything wayward. The last hole, at 542yd/496m par 5, needs three good shots, especially the generally underestimated approach. The well-bunkered, angled green

Above: An ancient aqueduct backs the 6th green, with the par-3 7th and wooded mountain scenery beyond. Below: The challenging 440yd/402m 16th is a demanding dogleg uphill that is rated the hardest par.

sits on a knoll falling away to the right and rear, and demands finesse and confidence.

This high-quality course was rewarded with the Portuguese Open in 1994 and 1995, as well as the Estoril Open in 1999.

9 *Mosteiro*

Caesar Park Penha Longa, Estrada da Lagoa Azul,
Linhó, 2710 Sintra
TEL: *(21) 924 9011* **FAX:** *(21) 924 9024*
LOCATION: *See Penha Longa, page 72*
COURSE: *9 holes, 2830yd/2588m, par 35, SSS 35*
TYPE OF COURSE: *Well-wooded rolling parkland
course with strategic lakes*
DESIGNER: *Robert Trent Jones Jr (1995)*
GREEN FEES: *EE*
FACILITIES: *Pro shop, cart, trolley, equipment and shoe
hire, golf academy tuition, driving range, putting green
and chipping practice area with bunker, changing
facilities, bar and restaurant in clubhouse*
VISITORS: *Welcome*

The latest addition to the Penha Longa resort, this attractive nine-hole course opened in 1995. It forms an interesting partner to the championship pedigree Atlantico. Designed to cater for a broader range of handicaps, the holes combine open parkland, some sloping fairways and three water holes, two of them par 3.

Recent reseeding of the fairways with rye grass has improved the condition of a course which winds through mature forest, passing historic ancient monuments and leisure sports facilities, in the northern sector of the estate. Apart from its architectural remains, Penha Longa (which means 'long rock') also has enormous natural outcrops, some featured on the golf courses.

The best hole is the 7th, an uphill par 4 of 377yd/345m. The drive needs to be held up to the right, as the fairway slopes severely left into sand, trees and out-of-bounds. The approach must carry to an elevated, blind green guarded by three large bunkers.

*The closing hole of Mosteiro has a fine view of the
ancient monastery church through the trees.*

10 *Marvão*

Club de Golf de Marvão, Quinta do Prado, S. Salvador
d'Aramenha, 7330 Marvão
TEL: *(245) 993755* **FAX:** *(245) 993805*
LOCATION: *8 miles/13km north-east of Portalegre on
N246*
COURSE: *18 holes, 6748yd/6170m, par 72, SSS 72*
TYPE OF COURSE: *Fairly level parkland with some
established trees and strategic water hazards*
DESIGNER: *Jorge Santana da Silva (1997)*
GREEN FEES: *E*
FACILITIES: *Pro shop, cart, trolley and equipment hire,
tuition, driving range, putting green, changing facilities,
bar and restaurant in clubhouse*
VISITORS: *Handicap certificate required*

Laid out below the historic clifftop town of Marvão and part of the São Mamede National Park, this new club is the most easterly in Portugal, not far from the border with Spain, and the first in the Alto Alentejo. Sited above the remains of an ancient Roman town, the club is less than 50 miles/80km from two Spanish counterparts, at Caceres and Badajoz. It is accessible from Badajoz International airport.

The course was designed by native Portuguese Jorge Santana da Silva, who also created the Amarante and Quinta da Barca courses to the north of Oporto. Essentially flat, it has three large lakes to facilitate drainage and irrigation, and to add strategic quality. Four holes, however, cover elevated land to the rear of the clubhouse and pose different problems. The most dramatic hole is probably the 17th, where an elevated tee shot seeks a green 219yd/200m away on a peninsula surrounded on three sides by water.

11 Beloura

Quinta da Beloura Golfe, Rua das Sesmarias 3, Estrada de Albarraque, 2710 Sintra
TEL: (21) 910 6350 **FAX:** (21) 910 6359
LOCATION: 3 miles/5k north of Estoril on N9 near Alcabideche
COURSE: 18 holes, 6362yd/5817m, par 73, SSS 71
TYPE OF COURSE: Gently sloping parkland laid out within an extensive housing development
DESIGNER: Rocky Roquemore (1994)
GREEN FEES: EE
FACILITIES: Pro shop, cart, trolley and equipment hire, tuition, driving range, putting green, changing rooms with sauna, jacuzzi, fitness room, bar and restaurant
VISITORS: Welcome

Having for far too long been a game with minority appeal to the domestic Portuguese market, golf is at last finding a foothold. Driving ranges and teaching schools are busier, appealing to both adults and children. Aware of this, the Beloura Golf Club has positioned itself as a cosmopolitan private club for golfing neophytes, and offers visitors fairly undemanding, uncluttered play, particularly midweek, at a reasonable price.

Laid out in 1994 as part of a burgeoning residential development, its fairways wander like green avenues through a new housing estate, where clusters of villas and apartments line each hole. With an industrialized perimeter, none would claim to visit for the view. But Beloura has much to offer, particularly for newer players. The course is kept in good condition, with over 40,000 new trees – oak, pine, palm, cedar and magnolia – due to enhance the future landscape.

12 Estoril-Sol

Academia Internacional de Golf Estoril-Sol, Quinta do Outeiro, Estrada da Lagoa Azul, Linhó, 2710 Sintra
TEL and FAX: (21) 923 2461
LOCATION: North of Estoril off N9 on road to Lagoa Azul
COURSE: 9 holes, 1913yd/1749m and 2034yd/1860m, each par 31
TYPE OF COURSE: Executive-style layout on steeply undulating land with lakes and mature trees
DESIGNERS: John Harris and Ronald Fream (1976)
GREEN FEES: E
FACILITIES: Pro shop, trolley and equipment hire, tuition, driving range, putting and approach greens in golf academy, changing facilities, bar and restaurant
VISITORS: Welcome

Originally built by the Estoril-Sol Hotel in 1976 as a short, very scenic nine-hole course in the shadow of the Sintra hills, the property has been extended and turned into to a fully fledged golf academy, managed by the Quinta da Marinha resort. In addition to the course itself, there is a full selection of practice tees and greens, bunkers and targets in one specific location, staffed by four professionals (two from Britain).

This establishment caters for the growing number of emergent local players, and is open to individuals, juniors and families, with special fees for limited membership. Although visiting golfers may play the nine-hole course on payment of a green fee, this is essentially a facility ideal for beginners, with overall levels of maintenance to match. However, for a brief round and a chance to sharpen up your short game, the pine-studded Estoril-Sol course offers an attractive and convenient opportunity.

Putting on the 9th/18th green at Estoril-Sol, one of several involving an accurate carry over water.

⛳ Estoril

Golf do Estoril, Avenida da República, 2765 Estoril
TEL: *(21) 468 0054* **FAX:** *(21) 468 2796*
E-MAIL: *cge@mail.telepac.pt*
LOCATION: *1 mile/2km north of Estoril on N9 to Sintra*
COURSE: *Championship: 18 holes, 5754yd/5262m, par 69, SSS 69; Blue: 9 holes, 2827yd/2585m, par 34*
TYPE OF COURSE: *Mature, well-wooded parkland course set on elevated, steeply undulating land with views of sea*
DESIGNER: *Mackenzie Ross (1945)*
GREEN FEES: *EE*
FACILITIES: *Pro shop, trolley and equipment hire, caddies, tuition, driving range, putting green, swimming pool, changing facilities, bar and restaurant*
VISITORS: *Welcome; handicap certificate required*

ESTORIL

HOLE	YD	M	PAR	HOLE	YD	M	PAR
1	385	352	4	10	502	459	5
2	156	143	3	11	415	379	4
3	319	292	4	12	339	310	4
4	177	162	3	13	167	153	3
5	517	473	5	14	396	362	4
6	266	243	4	15	326	298	4
7	419	383	4	16	201	184	3
8	215	197	3	17	297	272	4
9	379	346	4	18	278	254	4
OUT	2833	2591	34	IN	2921	2671	35

5754YD • 5262M • PAR 69

Some courses captivate on first aquaintance, infuriate with their subtle deceptions and remain totally and very fondly memorable. Clube de Golf do Estoril, *grande dame* and one of the longstanding gems of Portugal's golfing history, is just such a course. As a club with a pedigree, Estoril is everything you would expect. There is an aura of tradition from the moment you enter the old clubhouse – it is elegant, discreet, rich with the scent of old leather and history, timeless and ineffably Portuguese. Even though it is essentially a members' club, as a visitor you are made to feel more like an old family friend.

The club was founded in 1928 and moved to its present site in 1945. The Scottish designer who restored Turnberry, Mackenzie Ross, was presented with the challenge of conquering the steeply wooded slopes just above the seaside spa resort of Estoril, and succeeded in building a masterpiece. Although the course is not overlong by modern standards, it is highly strategic: a genuine test of finesse and skill, in an enchanting setting, that has stood the test of time.

One of the few clubs in Europe to retain a complement of caddies, many of them highly knowledgeable, Estoril was for many years the cornerstone of the game in Portugal. The resort, with its fashionable luxury hotels and casino, attracted European royalty, the well-connected or the merely wealthy, and the golf club formed an important social hub for Estoril's elite, mirroring the pattern set by Biarritz and Deauville in France. It was the annual home of the Portuguese Open and amateur championships for many years, and many leading professionals have tested their game here.

Accuracy is far more important than length, with the lush green fairways winding past ranks of eucalyptus and pine, often over quite severe gradients. The greens

are a delight, with smooth putting surfaces and subtle slopes. Playing the course, pitting your wits against the craft of the designer, is never less than a pleasure, especially in such scenic surroundings, with the breeze blowing off the sea far below, laden with the heady scent of mimosa.

Sadly there is always a price to pay for progress and the new motorway, while halving the driving time to Lisbon airport, has cut a concrete swathe through the course, forcing the redesign of two holes and the relocation of a third. However, only traditionalists could object to these sympathetic changes, which overall are probably an improvement.

Two of the best holes on the course are the 7th and 16th. The former is an uphill dogleg left of 419yd/383m, where the blind tee shot, over the corner of the hill, has to fight against the camber of the fairway, risking the trees on the left to avoid running into the rough on the right, with a demanding uphill shot to a well-protected plateau green to follow. The

The short 278yd/254m par-4 18th, a narrow uphill dogleg right, finishes right under the stately clubhouse, giving terrace diners a perfect grandstand view.

other is undoubtedly the par-3 16th, which, although amended to accommodate the motorway and shortened to a mere 201yd/184m, is still a classic and testing hole in a beautiful setting.

From here, the finish separates the men from the boys. Both holes are driveable for long hitters; both can ruin your score if you are slightly off line. Measured at 297yd/272m and 278yd/254m respectively, the holes can tempt the gambler in you. It's easy to play safe off the tee, although this does not guarantee a clear second to the green, such is the strategic placement of trees and sand, but it is difficult to resist the lure of back-to-back birdies.

The restaurant upstairs in the clubhouse offers timeless service and cuisine, while the view from the shaded balcony of the uphill sweep of the 18th, with the sparkling sea beyond, is unmatched.

Quinta da Marinha

Quinta da Marinha Hotel Village Resort, Casa 36, 2750 Cascais
TEL: *(21) 486 9881/9* **FAX:** *(21) 486 9032*
E-MAIL: *marinhagolf@mail.telepac.pt*
LOCATION: *3 miles/5km west of Cascais on N247*
COURSE: *18 holes, 6577yd/6014m, par 71, SSS 71*
TYPE OF COURSE: *Fairly level combination of park and heathland with several lakes and sea views*
DESIGNER: *Robert Trent Jones (1984)*
GREEN FEES: *EE*
FACILITIES: *Pro shop, cart, trolley and equipment hire, tuition, driving range and putting green, tennis courts, swimming pools, changing facilities, bar and restaurant in clubhouse*
VISITORS: *Welcome; regular handicap required for weekend and holiday play*

QUINTA DA MARINHA

HOLE	YD	M	PAR	HOLE	YD	M	PAR
1	582	532	5	10	537	491	5
2	145	133	3	11	590	540	5
3	569	520	5	12	451	412	4
4	393	359	4	13	426	390	4
5	169	155	3	14	159	145	3
6	537	491	5	15	359	328	4
7	166	152	3	16	159	145	3
8	410	375	4	17	365	334	4
9	182	166	3	18	378	346	4
OUT	3153	2883	35	IN	3424	3131	36

6577YD • 6014M • PAR 71

Laid out over a relatively level site with some mature pine trees, views of the sea on one side and the distant Sintra mountains on the other, the Quinta da Marinha resort would appear to have the ideal ingredients. Add in a tennis complex with nine courts (three floodlit), two swimming pools, a large estate village of rustic townhouses and villas (many for rent) tucked away under pine trees, an ancient royal hunting lodge for a clubhouse and an 18-hole golf course designed by the American master architect Robert Trent Jones, and few would ask for more.

Yet, since its opening in 1984, Quinta da Marinha has somehow always seemed to promise more than it could deliver. It has tended to disappoint many through poor course condition, long walks from green to tee, a lack of cohesive flow in the layout, intrusive housing, overhead cables and protective netting plus a general inattention to detail. The course seems to have had a lower priority, both for land and budget, than other elements such as the real estate, and has suffered from a continuing lack of investment.

It was clearly difficult to fit a major golf course project into the land available – pine woods running down past indigenous heathland to ravines and clifftops overlooking the ocean. The site is attractive but the opportunity so far unfulfilled.

Fortunately, salvation appears to be at hand. A new 200-bed hotel opened on the inland edge of the course at the end of 1999. The four-star Marinha Golf Hotel has indoor and outdoor swimming pools, massage and sauna in its health centre, conference facilities and – a novel feature – reserved overnight parking in its basement for golfing guests' buggies, hired by the week.

In tandem with the opening of the hotel, major refurbishment projects are in hand on the golf course. Under the supervision of a new greenkeeper, the work includes total renewal of the greens, reconstruction of all tees, fairway reseeding with Bermuda, changes to the irrigation system, revised drainage and new sand in the bunkers, plus waterproofing of all lakes. Such modifications and improvements should satisfy most concerns about the course and create a layout whose playing conditions are on a par with any in the area, with the added benefit of a superb coastal location.

All visitors recall the dramatic par-3 14th, played across a deep rocky gorge overlooking the sea, but the two most strategic and demanding holes, each 537yd/491m long and double-doglegged, are the 6th and 10th. At the former, the hole bears left, leaving a second shot to a narrowing fairway with out-of-bounds on both sides, before turning right towards a split-level, heavily bunkered green. The 10th, a mirror-image of the 6th, is dominated by two large lakes, the first to the right, the second on the left. You must keep

The 13th curves majestically downhill right towards a shelf of green, seemingly hanging over the ocean.

The 15th is shortish but easy to leak your drive left. Your shot to the shallow, angled green must be perfect.

left off the tee but long enough to carry over the narrow strip linking the two water hazards while avoiding a bunker complex. The green – small, shallow and steeply elevated – is a tight target on the left-hand side nudging into the lake. These are two holes to treat with the utmost respect.

Pass the Port

The history and progress of golf in Portugal is undeniably British, started by expatriate wine shippers in Oporto in the 19th century. And little seems more quintessentially British than their prime commodity (and no doubt tipple) – port. Generally regarded as the queen of fortified wines, port has maintained strong links with golf and golfers ever since, as well as providing the cue for generations of after-dinner speakers.

The drink, with its unique combination of fruit, alcohol and sweetness, has been produced in the Douro region since the early British houses, Croft and Taylors among others, set up shop in the late 1600s and began adding brandy to wine to preserve it on the long sea-voyage to Britain. Oporto remains the focal point for a trade that is as

The Douro River winds down to Oporto past the terraced vineyards of Taylors, one of the original port wine shippers and still amongst the leaders.

vibrant today as ever, still dominated by the grand old British firms and meeting worldwide demand from a single region of northern Portugal. Port accounts for only 7.5 million cases out of the country's total wine production of 100 million.

A total of 80,000 vineyards cover 60,000 acres/24,000ha, many steeply terraced along the banks of the Douro River. There are 48 authorized grape varieties available to create the rich, warm, spicy nectar, often deeply coloured, evoking images of nuts, brown sugar, raisins, liquorice, tobacco, pepper, herbs and plums. It is a drink of undoubted class and pedigree, improved with age.

You can choose from ruby, tawny, crusted, late-bottled vintage, single quinta or vintage. The latter is the finest, only offered from 'declared' years, matured in oak casks for two years and then ideally developed in bottle for a further 15–25 years. Portugal's gift has warmed and cheered many a golfer in the past and looks set to do so for years to come.

15 Vimeiro

Termas do Vimeiro, Praia de Porto Novo, 2650 Torres Vedras
TEL: *(261) 984157* **FAX:** *(261) 984621*
LOCATION: *10 miles/16km north of Torres Vedras, off N8-2*
COURSE: *9 holes, 5229yd/4781m, par 67, SSS 67*
TYPE OF COURSE: *Level parkland holes on a compact site inland from the sea*
DESIGNER: *Frank Pennink (1963)*
GREEN FEES: *E*
FACILITIES: *Equipment and trolley hire, changing facilities, outdoor and indoor swimming pools in hotel, tennis and access to beach, bar, restaurant*
VISITORS: *Welcome*

Vimeiro, a nine-hole course which forms part of the spa hotel complex of the same name, is what true vacation golf should be. Nine level holes (after the spectacular opening shot from an elevated tee outside the hotel itself) are beautifully maintained – especially the greens – and full of interest.

Frank Pennink, who designed the course in 1963, was faced with squeezing nine holes into the space behind the clifftop hotel, which enjoys fine sea views. Rows of bushy trees border the quite narrow fairways and the broad Alcabrichel River bisects the site, potentially affecting play on four holes. As part of a seaside holiday location, it offers relatively undemanding golf to be enjoyed free by hotel guests of all abilities in a most attractive setting. Beyond the hotel is an excellent beach, and inland you can explore Torres Vedras, linked with Wellington and the Napoleonic War.

16 Botado

Complexo Turistico do Botado, Praia da Consolação, 2520 Peniche
TEL: *(262) 757700* **FAX:** *(262) 750717*
LOCATION: *4 miles/6km south of Peniche off N247*
COURSE: *9 holes, 5292yd/4839m, alternate tees, par 72, SSS 72*
TYPE OF COURSE: *Fairly level sandy duneland by the sea with many lakes and juniper bushes*
DESIGNER: *Mateus Marteleira (1996)*
GREEN FEES: *E*
FACILITIES: *Hotel, golf shop, cart, trolley and equipment hire, driving range, putting green, changing facilities, bar, restaurant*
VISITORS: *Welcome*

Something of a curiosity but located in a setting of substantial natural beauty, this rustic nine-hole course has been developed over gently undulating duneland between the Atlantico Golf Hotel and the sea, primarily as a facility for hotel guests. It offers an interesting, if rather short, test over fairly unmanicured sandy seaside terrain.

Water (there are seven water hazards, affecting shots on every hole) and large waste sand areas have an important part to play on a course which also incorporates a protected juniper grove. Accuracy rather than length is required at Botado, since there are a large number of unplayable lies. The well-appointed four-star hotel acts as clubhouse and so can offer above average bar and restaurant facilities. Staying here provides a seaside centre for a holiday, and a base for touring Peniche, Obidos and Caldas da Rainha.

Putting on the 1st/10th green with the Vimeiro hotel, the site of the hole's unusual tee-off location, in the rear.

17 Praia d'El Rey

Praia d'El Rey Golf & Country Club, Vale de Janelas, Apartado 2, 2510 Obidos
TEL: *(262) 905005* **FAX:** *(262) 905009*
E-MAIL: *educla@mail.telepac.pt*
LOCATION: *15 miles/25km west of Obidos, via N114 to Peniche, turning right at Serra d'El Rey*
COURSE: *18 holes, 7072yd/6467m, par 72, SSS 72*
TYPE OF COURSE: *A unique combination of seaside linksland, including high dunes, and rolling sandy heathland with mature pines*
DESIGNER: *Cabell Robinson (1997)*
GREEN FEES: *EEE*
FACILITIES: *Pro shop, cart, trolley and equipment hire, tuition, driving range, putting green and chipping practice area, swimming pool, changing facilities, snack bar, bar, restaurant*
VISITORS: *Welcome; soft spikes only*

	PRAIA D'EL REY						
HOLE	YD	M	PAR	HOLE	YD	M	PAR
1	421	385	4	10	525	480	5
2	506	463	5	11	200	183	3
3	183	167	3	12	396	362	4
4	332	304	4	13	328	300	4
5	482	441	4	14	164	150	3
6	395	361	4	15	436	399	4
7	568	519	5	16	467	427	4
8	184	168	3	17	623	570	5
9	430	393	4	18	432	395	4
OUT	3501	3201	36	IN	3571	3266	36

7072YD • 6467M • PAR 72

It is quite rare for a new golf development to run down to and along a pristine sandy shoreline. It is even rarer for the seaside location to be annexed by the golf course, rather than allocated for hotel or private housing projects. In Praia d'El Rey, a superb new course created in 1997, the far-sighted developers have realized the true potential of the rugged sandy duneland along the 1.5 miles/2.5km beach and devoted it to golf. In doing so, they have allowed the architect (with considerable help from nature) to fashion a magnificent links test: undoubtedly the best seaside course in Portugal and arguably one of the best half-dozen in continental Europe. To underline its class, the club has twice hosted the European Cup, the match between the top European ladies and senior men professionals.

The golf course flows past high sand dunes, along the beach and inland to some wooded, parkland-style holes, making a course of contrasts, blessed with some of the finest natural links terrain any designer could wish for. From the elevated, centrally sited clubhouse and on some high points of the course, there are magnificent views to the sea and along the coast. The location, in the south-eastern corner of the Costa de Prata near the beautifully preserved medieval town of Obidos, is ruggedly unspoiled yet reachable in an hour by car from Lisbon.

The development is still in its early stages. Near the attractive single-storey clubhouse there is floodlit tennis, plus opportunities for watersports, game fishing and diving, and an equestrian centre.

As befits what is essentially a links course, there is little strategic water (apart, of course, from the Atlantic Ocean) but sufficient rough, gorse, sea grass and waste sand areas to demand accuracy. The fairways are generous, although landing areas can be tight for the par player. The key to a good score lies in the back nine, where the sea

breeze plays a significant part. The 11th (see page 4) is a good one-shotter, 200yd/183m from the back, usually downwind but steeply uphill to a small green ringed by juniper bushes. The view from the elevated tee of the 396yd/362m 12th, straight out to sea over a fairway winding through the dunes, is enough to distract anyone.

The three holes that follow run right along the shore, reasonably straightforward in themselves but open to the capricious nature of any coastal wind. Then you turn for home and discover the sting in Praia d'El Rey's tail. The 16th is a strong par 4, 467yd/427m from the back tee and all uphill. It is followed by the third longest par 5 in Portugal – 623yd/570m curving left – a hole full of choices where you need to know your game (see page 55). After that, the 432yd/395m 18th might seem a relief but there are blind carries and a small, well-protected green set in amongst dunes to complete a genuine championship test.

Above: Running right along the seashore, the 328yd/300m 13th, open to any breeze, represents true links golf.
Below: A superb dogleg left par 4 with a view, the 12th offers choices and is a gambler's hole.

Golden Eagle

Golden Eagle Golf and Country Club, Quinta do
Brinçal, Arrouquelas, 2040 Rio Maior
TEL: *(243) 908148* FAX: *(243) 908149*
LOCATION: *39 miles/63km north of Lisbon on IC2,
south of Rio Maior*
COURSE: *18 holes, 6558yd/5997m, par 72, SSS 72*
TYPE OF COURSE: *Rolling heathland with some
elevated tees, lakes and mature trees*
DESIGNER: *Rocky Roquemore (1994)*
GREEN FEES: *EE*
FACILITIES: *Pro shop, trolleys, tuition, driving range,
putting green, changing facilities, bar, restaurant*
VISITORS: *Welcome with prior reservation*

GOLDEN EAGLE

HOLE	YD	M	PAR	HOLE	YD	M	PAR
1	525	480	5	10	387	354	4
2	163	149	3	11	142	130	3
3	430	393	4	12	358	327	4
4	349	319	4	13	356	326	4
5	219	200	3	14	498	455	5
6	387	354	4	15	178	163	3
7	537	491	5	16	379	347	4
8	408	373	4	17	409	374	4
9	462	423	5	18	371	339	4
OUT	3480	3182	37	IN	3078	2815	35

6558YD • 5997M • PAR 72

Golden Eagle has remained a well-kept secret for far too long. Tucked away inland among gently undulating wooded slopes and heathland areas, it is about an hour's drive from Lisbon. Recently, a more liberal attitude to visitors to the club has allowed more golfers to discover the charms and challenges of a course laid out in 1994 in a spectacular location.

This is another design from the prolific American architect Rocky Roquemore, and arguably one of his best. As at Quinta do Perú (see page 64), he was offered a site of dramatic natural beauty, with well-established pine forests, eucalyptus and acacia, much natural flora carpeting the sandy landscape and some sensational changes of elevation. The landscape echoes the English wooded splendours of Wentworth and Sunningdale plus the open charms of Walton Heath; the design characteristics here, however, are strictly US modern, though they are in total sympathy with the terrain.

The club was for some years deliberately exclusive, a peaceful haven open only to its members and their guests. It developed an aura of mystique, with a word-of-mouth reputation for quality but also inaccessibility, except to a privileged few. It was a frustrating situation, especially in a country not exactly overloaded with courses of international class. However, recent changes of policy, coupled with improvements to the motorway system north of Lisbon, have allowed greater access for visiting players.

Set in splendid isolation, the course has numerous lakes and large areas of white sand, which contrast with the background of mature pine, silver birch, acacias and native flora. Despite its comparative youth, it has an air of permanence, each hole securely settled in its very natural location. One feature, unusual in courses of the modern era, is that you do not pass by the clubhouse after nine holes, but

Above: Teeshot view of the short 11th, serenely sited over water. Below: The high tee and heathland setting of the 358yd/327m 12th typifies Golden Eagle's terrain.

return only after the round is completed.

All the holes are interesting, most making good use of the natural terrain to pose questions. The high point, literally, is the short 5th, where the green lies 219yd/200m steeply below the tee, well protected by sand and surrounding slopes. Whatever your score here, enjoy the fantastic view. The 7th hole, 537yd/491m par 5, is a double dogleg which appears as a sea of sand from the tee, with no less than 11 bunkers to be negotiated.

Water, rather than sand, affects play on the 10th and 11th. The former is a dogleg right par 4 of 387yd/354m, where you thread your way between the right-hand lake and sand, then have to carry the corner of the lake to hold a small green. The 142yd/130m par 3 that follows looks innocuous but with water in front and sand beyond, requires precise club selection to reach a shallow green in a sheltered corner of the course. There is plenty of variety here, in both terrain and design, and a genuine test of shotmaking in a tranquil setting that you feel privileged to enjoy.

The rustic wooden clubhouse has a patio area looking down on the first tee and a pleasant bar and restaurant with a notable wine list. Golden Eagle's secrets are well worth examination.

REGIONAL DIRECTORY

Where to Stay

Lisbon **Dom Pedro Lisboa** (21 389 6600, Fax 21 389 6601) The newest 5-star hotel in the city is also sited at its heart, 20 minutes from the international airport. A modern 21-floor building with excellent views, it has 263 opulently furnished rooms. The hotel has three restaurants – one Italian, a café and bistro – plus barber shop, hairdresser, gymnasium, sauna, solarium and an extensive range of shops. Well-placed for sightseeing, shopping, excellent restaurants and nightlife, it is also equidistant from most of the golf in the region.

Estoril **Hotel Palacio** (21 468 0400, Fax 21 468 4867) The epitome of elegance, this long-established 5-star luxury hotel sits in palatial splendour facing the tropical gardens and grand casino. Traditional in every sense, its tasteful public rooms and faultless service recall a bygone era. There are two restaurants, including the highly recommended Four Seasons Grill, a hairdresser, barber shop, sauna and large outdoor pool. Guests enjoy reduced fees at the hotel's own 18-hole golf course (see pages 76/77) and access to the Estoril Tennis Club next door.

Sintra **Caesar Park** (21 924 9011, Fax 21 924 9007) A magnificent hotel in a peerl;ess setting on the wooded 600 acre/240ha Penha Longa estate. It overlooks both golf courses and the 14th-century monastery, palace and church. Luxury and impeccable service are a feature at every turn with international and Japanese cuisine plus a further restaurant in the golf club, an extensive health club, indoor and outdoor swimming pools, sauna and massage, gymnasium and hairdresser. There are also tennis courts and cycles to explore the many historic features of the Penha Longa property.

Obidos **Pousada de Castelo** (262 959105, Fax 262 959148) A superbly preserved castle captured from the Moors by Portugal's first monarch, Dom Afonso Henriques, in the 12th century and now restored and converted into a *pousada*, one of the national network of state-owned heritage hotels. It has only six rooms and three suites but each is beautifully appointed, leaving visitors with the feeling of being favoured guests in an ancestral home. Decor is traditional and the restaurant, which boasts an interesting menu, including braised kid and grilled bass with baked potatoes, has an ancestral ambience in keeping with its location.

Palmela **Pousada de Palmela** (21 235 1226, Fax 21 233 0440) This medieval castle occupies the hilltop of this ancient village. It was conquered by the Moors in the 12th century, then transformed into a convent in the 15th. It has now been rebuilt and remodelled as a *pousada,* where the old

cloisters, stone stairs and tapestried halls lend considerable atmosphere. It has 27 rooms and one suite, with superb views and an elegant restaurant offering such delights as trout stuffed with Montijo ham and pears stewed with local Moscatel wine.

Sesimbra **Hotel do Mar** (21 223 3326, Fax 21 223 3888) This is a deceptively spacious hotel, built into the hillside overlooking the delightful fishing village of Sesimbra, with its many small seafood restaurants. There are 169 comfortable rooms, all with sea view, reached unusually from a reception entrance on the top floor. There are outdoor and indoor heated swimming pools, tennis and access to watersports. The setting is picturesque and only a few steps from the sea front.

Where to Eat

Lisbon Visit **Aviz** (21 385 1888) for a step back in time, with service and cuisine to match. **Tagide** (21 342 1112) offers a classic quality menu with a panoramic view over Lisbon and the Tagus River. **York House** (21 396 2435) is in a 16th-century convent with high quality service and menu in a garden setting. For a taste of local culture, dine at **A Severa** (21 342 8314) on authentic Portuguese specialities with regional dance and typical *fado* performances included.

Estoril/Cascais/Guimcho **Sentinela da Noite** (21 468 7364) offers Portuguese cooking, particularly shellfish, plus a good wine list. **Os Arcos** (21 443 3374) is in a pleasant situation, specializing in fish and seafood. **Casa Velha** (21 483 2586) has a friendly atmosphere with a popular Portuguese menu. **O Pescador** (21 483 2054) serves international cuisine with excellent fish. **Panorama** (21 487 0062) offers Portuguese specialities and friendly service by the sea. **Monte-Mar** (21 486 9270) is the ultimate in dining out in style with ocean views and an expensive international menu. **Portal da Guia** (21 464 3258), on the Guincho coast, serves a range of Portuguese specialities.

Obidos **O Caldeiro** (262 959839) is comfortable and friendly, with an interesting menu.

Setubal **Novo Reno** (265 30115) is small, friendly and very Portuguese, with fresh fish and reasonable prices. **A Caso do Xico** (265 39502) is a popular restaurant specializing in grilled fish.

Sesimbra **Tony Bar** (21 223 3199) specializes in grilled fish and seafood and is very popular with visiting tourists. **Ribamar** (21 223 4853) has long experience in regional cuisine, with good support from the locals. **O Esconolidnho** (21 223 3480) is noted for its friendly atmosphere and good home cooking. **Pedra Alta** (21 223 1791) faces the sea, and has a well-deserved reputation for its grilled fish.

What to See

There is plenty of evidence of the long and turbulent history of Lisbon and its surrounding regions, the centre of one of the oldest nations in Europe. The city has been successively occupied since 1200 BC by Phoenicians, Greeks, Carthaginians, Romans, Visigoths and Moors, a historic blend visible in architecture, culture and cuisine. Finally, with the assistance of English crusaders, the country's first king, Don Afonso Henriques, conquered the 'delightful little port', tumbling down from a series of hills to the banks of the River Tagus, in 1147, to establish the nation's capital. Close to the Atlantic and with a long maritime tradition, Lisbon became an important port from the 15th century onwards, receiving the rewards of the global exploration of its seafaring pioneers. The earthquake of 1755 destroyed much of the city and provided the Marquis of Pombal with the opportunity to oversee the rebuilding of the city in the elegant form that survives today.

In **Lisbon**, start with the **Castle of São Jorge**. Julius Caesar supposedly slept here but most come for the breathtaking view out over the city and its river. **Belem** is marked by the waterside fortified tower of the same name, built in the 16th century as a tribute to the country's courageous navigators who charted the globe and now a UNESCO World Heritage site. Its Moorish-influenced design is in stark contrast to the modern **Monument to the Discoveries** a short distance away, constructed in 1960 to commemorate the 500th anniversary of Prince Henry the Navigator's death. Close by is the **Monastery of the Hieronymites**, begun in 1502. Its superbly delicate Manueline architecture includes the tombs of explorer Vasco de Gama and Portugal's greatest poet Luis de Camões. Another Belem landmark is

Built to withstand attack, the fortified walls of Obidos encircle a medieval village of great charm and interest, little changed over the centuries.

the **National Coach Museum**, next to the president's palace. Many elegant examples of horse-drawn coachwork in a gilded setting evoke the spirit of more graceful times.

En route to **Estoril**, visit the **National Palace of Queluz**, which is a fine example of the 18th-century neoclassical style, with tastefully decorated salons and formal gardens. Then on to **Sintra** and the grandeur of the **National Palace**, the summer residence of Portuguese royalty since the 14th century and rich with the overlay of different reigns. Here also is the **Castle of the Moors** (7th to 9th centuries) and the exotic **Pena Palace** on the mountain peak, rebuilt and extravagantly restored in the 19th century by Don Fernando II. An interesting feature just beyond Cascais is the **Boca do Inferno** ('Mouth of Hell'), where incoming waves pound through a natural opening in the cliff face, with dramatic effect.

To the north, take time to explore **Obidos**, a rare example of a medieval fortified town, the towering castle and maze of streets winding past whitewashed houses; all enclosed by the original battlemented walls: a step back in time and a unique experience.

In the Costa Azul to the south, stop in **Azeitão** where one of the country's leading winemakers, the firm of Jose Maria da Fonseca, produce a wide variety of high quality red and white wines and offer guided tours and tastings. Finally, while descending to **Sesimbra**, find time to turn off and explore the ruined Moorish castle, with its old church and museum, high above this quaint fishing village.

Chapter 3

The North

A visit to the north of Portugal, the Costa Verde or Green Coast, is like a step back in time. Although the main city, Oporto, is the second most important in the country, this is a region steeped in history and local tradition, where the tide of tourism has so far had little noticeable effect. The region is more green because of its northerly location and greater rainfall. The average summer temperature of 68°F/20°C drops to a cool average of 48°F/9°C in winter.

From Atlantic beaches to inland mountains, this relatively unspoiled area can claim to be Portugal's oldest region. This is where the country began, at Guimarães in the 12th century and also, coincidentally, where the first golfers tackled the sea breezes at Espinho in 1890. Much evidence remains of Celtic, Roman and later cultural influences: in the local dances and songs, sturdy stone bridges, medieval castles, great baroque cathedrals and palaces, as well as the wealth of historic mansions and manor houses, many of which now offer tourist accommodation and warm hospitality.

Left: The classic lines of the Don Luis I road bridge, built in 1886, form an Oporto landmark. Above: Old windmills are a feature of the north.

The focal point has to be Oporto, linked by motorway to Lisbon and with its own international airport. The city clings to the sloping banks of the Douro River, which winds through a verdant landscape of steep terraced vineyards, birthplace of the wines for which the region is world famous. No visitor should miss the abundance of fine art and architecture in the Romanesque-Gothic cathedral, the many churches and the 18th-century Baroque Torre dos Clérigos, which dominates the city's skyline. Equally, the wine cellars of the great port lodges at Vila Nova de Gaia provide a link with the past, as well as free tastings.

Apart from port, shoppers will admire the craftsmanship in intricate gold and silver filigree work as well as the range of painstaking hand embroidery, lace and tapestry. Golfers venturing to Ponte de Lima will find basketwork, *vinho verde* and lacework a speciality while Viana do Castelo, just down the road, is noted for its handicrafts, embroideries and colourful regional costumes, which are best seen at one of the many religious festivals held through the year. Those who fancy a flutter can follow horse racing at Ponte de

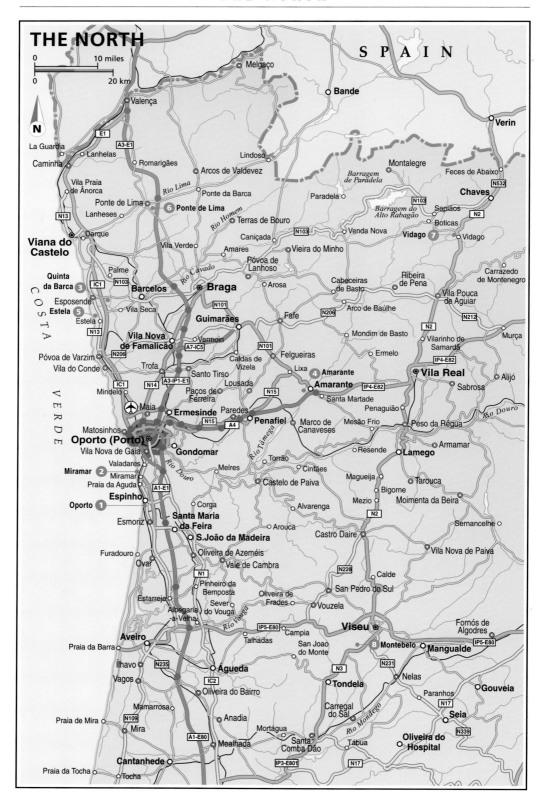

Lima or visit the casino at Póvoa de Varzim, near Estela.

Further afield, Guimarães has the impressive castle of Portugal's first king, Don Afonso Henriques, the palace of the Dukes of Bragança and the medieval Museu Alberto Sampaio. Barcelos has a walled town and dungeon dating from medieval times. Bragança is another ancient town with much to see within its castellated walls, including 16th-century churches and a railway museum.

The Costa Verde is noted for its cuisine, which is strongly influenced by the local produce and the prevailing climate. Expect hearty soups, rich stews based on pork or veal and beans, spicy sausage, tripe and potatoes. Typical dishes include *caldo verde*, a soup of green cabbage, potatoes and sausage; *bacalhau* (salt cod) prepared in a variety of ways (see panel); freshwater trout; roasted or stewed meats; various sweetmeats based on egg yolks, quince, custard, honey and flaky pastry; rice pudding, candied almonds and roast chestnuts.

The natural complement will be the local wines, whether the fresh young *vinho*

An ancient bridge leads into the delightful small town of Arcos de Valdevez in the Minho.

verde, red or white, or the excellent table wines from the Douro valley. Chilled white port is drunk as an aperitif and the glorious range of rich deep port vintages as post-prandial nectar (see page 80).

BACALHAU: THE FAITHFUL FRIEND

Bacalhau is cod – which in Portugal means salt cod – and is rightly regarded as the Portuguese national dish. It is reputed to have 365 different methods of preparation. Originally dried and salted as a means of preservation on long sea voyages, this method of preparation continues today as the Portuguese adore salt cod, calling it *fiel amigo* ('faithful friend'), and the dried fish hangs in stiff rows in local shops, where it is available in a range of different grades. Recipes include *pasteis de bacalhau* (salted cod cakes), *empadao de bacalhau* (salted cod pie), *meia-desfeita com grão* (boiled cod and chickpeas), *assado no forno* (oven-roasted) and the quintessential Christmas Eve dish, *bacalhau cozido com todos* (cod cooked with everything).

 Oporto

Oporto Golf Club, Lugar do Sisto, Paramos, 4500
Espinho
TEL: *(22) 734 2008* **FAX:** *(22) 734 6895*
LOCATION: *On south side of Espinho, 9 miles/14km
south of Oporto on N109*
COURSE: *6135yd/5610m, par 71, SSS 70*
TYPE OF COURSE: *True links by the sea with dunes
and sandhills; few trees*
DESIGNER: *Unknown (1890)*
GREEN FEES: *EE*
FACILITIES: *Pro shop, trolley and equipment hire,
caddies, tuition, driving range, putting green, changing
facilities, snack bar, bar, restaurant*
VISITORS: *Handicap certificate and proper attire
required. Reservations necessary. Tee-off weekends and
holidays before 10.30 if no competition. Restaurant
terrace and living room for members only at weekends and
holidays; visitors' light meals in bar*

Golfing visitors to Portugal can enjoy a
wide selection of fine courses, mostly
created in the last 30 years and often reflecting
the latest techniques of course construction
and design; many are aimed specifically at
holiday players. You should not, however,
ignore the origins of the game in Portugal and
the historic links of the Oporto Golf Club,
where it all began. A visit here can put the
development of the game in perspective and,
to some extent, it still offers an opportunity to

*The surroundings of the 9th green typify this historic
traditional links course, where seagrass, massive sand
dunes and the ocean breeze are constant hazards.*

experience golf as it used to be played more
than a century ago.

The course was created in 1890 on a stretch
of sandy linksland just south of Oporto by a
group of British wine shippers who wanted to
enjoy their time-honoured game. The oldest in
Portugal, the club ranks fourth in Continental
Europe after Pau (1856) and the clubs of
Biarritz and Royal Antwerp (both 1888). It
offers 18 holes of original links golf, seemingly
unaffected by the passing of the years.

The club is strong on tradition and this is
reflected in the course. The narrow fairways
wind past areas of sand and seagrass, low
dunes and scrub bushes, played in a prevailing
northerly wind. There are echoes of the
courses of Royal North Devon and Royal
West Norfolk in England, and it appears
frozen in time, so that you almost expect to
round a sandhill and meet some of the
original members wielding hickory clubs.

The clubhouse is discreet, single-storey and
full of historic memorabilia. Its restaurant has
a considerable reputation.

Miramar

Club de Golf de Miramar, Avenida Sacadura Cabral,
Praia de Miramar, 4405 Valadares
TEL: *(22) 762 2067* **FAX:** *(22) 762 7859*
LOCATION: *6 miles/10km south of Oporto on N109*
COURSE: *9 holes, 2814yd/2573m, par 68, SSS 67*
TYPE OF COURSE: *Mature, fairly level course beside
the sea with some dunes*
DESIGNERS: *Frank Gordon and Arthur Mariani (1932)*
GREEN FEES: *9 holes E; 18 holes EE*
FACILITIES: *Golf shop, trolley and equipment hire,
caddies, driving range, chipping practice area and
putting greens, changing facilities, swimming pool,
bar, restaurant*
VISITORS: *Welcome*

There is always a warm welcome for the
visitor to this, one of Portugal's most
venerable private clubs. Opened in 1932,
Miramar is a delightful nine-hole course on a
compact site of gently undulating, sandy
linksland near the sea. The holes are well
crafted and reward thoughtful play, with
sand, mature conifers and regular sea breezes
adding to the interest.

Despite its years, there are holes here to
appeal to all players' skills, most notably the
9th, a 392yd/358m par 4 with out-of-
bounds all along the right-hand side of its
narrow fairway, trees to the left and a fast
well-defended green at the finish in front of
the friendly clubhouse. Although the course
is protected from the sea
by low dunes, there are
magnificent views from
the higher tees to the
beach and sea. Kept in
excellent condition, this is
a links location that will
reward a visit.

*The green of the 302yd/276m
par-4 3rd hole at Miramar, the
furthest point from the clubhouse,
is backed by high dunes: welcome
protection from the sea.*

 Quinta da Barca

Golfe da Quinta da Barca, Barca do Lago, 4740
Esposende
TEL: *(253) 966723* **FAX:** *(253) 969068*
LOCATION: *30 miles/48km north of Oporto on N13
north of Fão bridge*
COURSE: *9 holes, 2201yd/2012m, par 31*
TYPE OF COURSE: *Level circuit with large greens and
mature pines*
DESIGNER: *Jorge Santana da Silva (1997)*
GREEN FEES: *EE*
FACILITIES: *Golf shop, trolley and equipment hire,
tuition, driving range, putting and pitching greens,
changing facilities, bar, snack bar, restaurant*
VISITORS: *Welcome*

Created in 1997 as a nine-hole course to
cater for the occupants of a tourist and
residential complex, the layout, by the
Portuguese designer Jorge Santana da Silva,
completely circumnavigates the development.
Set on one bank of the Cavado River at Barca
do Lago, just south of the coastal town of
Esposende, here is a small golfing gem to seek
out and enjoy. Well-designed, with artfully
shaped, well-mounded greens and a number
of water hazards, the holes thread their way
past tall stands of pine and lavish splashes of
sand. It will perhaps not appeal to all, but for
those who value precision over length and
appreciate a gentle stroll in a relaxed and
charming locale, it has a lot to offer.

 *Amarante*

Amarante Golf Clube, Lugar da Devesa, Fregim, 4600 Amarante
TEL: *(255) 446060* **FAX:** *(255) 446202*
LOCATION: *38 miles/56km east of Oporto at Louredo, off N210 north of Amarante*
COURSE: *18 holes, 5563yd/5085m, par 68, SSS 68*
TYPE OF COURSE: *Well-wooded mountain course with some spectacular holes and views*
DESIGNER: *Jorge Santana da Silva (1997)*
GREEN FEES: *EE*
FACILITIES: *Golf shop, cart, trolley and equipment hire, tuition, driving range, pitching and putting greens, tennis, swimming pools, sauna, changing facilities, bar, restaurant*
VISITORS: *Welcome*

Golf laid out over level land is normally easy to create but often rather uninspiring to the eye. However, projects which attempt to turn mountainsides into courses can offer spectacular views but also holes which require blind faith and much local knowledge to avoid disaster. The Quinta da Devesa course is one of the latter, having only recently opened on hilly terrain rising 1970ft/600m above sea level.

There is little doubt that the project posed a considerable challenge to designer Jorge Santana da Silva, since the steeply wooded slopes of the Amarante hill and limited suitable land area necessitated narrow angled fairways and small, often severely elevated, greens.

The card of 5563yd/5085m may well be a strict par 68 but, with a number of blind approaches and dramatic changes in elevation, the first-time visitor will be tested all the way. Lakes play a major role at the tight downhill-dogleg par-4 3rd hole and the one-shot 13th, where both greens require a precise approach if penal water is to be avoided. In an attempt to maximize the use of the limited land available, the architect has introduced two pairs of double fairways linking the 8th and 18th as well as the 5th and 14th holes, the latter on two distinct plateaux.

Amarante presents an exciting, adventurous test of shotmaking over some demanding terrain, with severe penalties for shots off line. There are also great views to the distant mountains of Aboboreira and Marão. For all but the fittest, the use of a golf cart is recommended.

Length is not the problem on the steeply downhill par-3 15th; it is the magnetic out-of-bounds left and sand beyond.

 Estela

Estela Golfe Clube, Rio Alto, Estela, 4490 Póvoa de Varzim
TEL: *(252) 601567* **FAX:** *(252) 612701*
LOCATION: *26 miles/40km north of Oporto on N13*
COURSE: *18 holes, 6580yd/6017m, par 72, SSS 73*
TYPE OF COURSE: *Two narrow loops of linksland running parallel to the beach and sea*
DESIGNER: *Duarte Sottomayor (1989)*
GREEN FEES: *EE*
FACILITIES: *Golf shop, cart, trolley and equipment hire. tuition, driving range, putting green, changing facilities, sauna, beach, snack bar, bar and restaurant in clubhouse*
VISITORS: *Welcome except during competitions*

Genuine links golf courses outside Great Britain and Ireland are rare, especially those built in recent years. The Estela course falls yet somehow fails to come into this category. Sandwiched into a long narrow site bordering 2 miles/3km of undeveloped beach, its fairways squeeze past dunes and hillocks of waste sand like so many canned green sardines. Nine holes run out to either side of the central

The opening drive establishes the course: only 485yd/ 443m par 5 but narrow, winding past dunes and scrub with a sea breeze.

clubhouse, with the Atlantic on one side and rather unattractive surroundings inland.

The designer, Duarte Sottomayor, was presented with a classic linksland situation but failed to grasp the opportunity. Lush Bermuda fairways, several water hazards and mostly well-elevated bent grass greens seem out of character in a links setting. The latter particularly, since they demand high-trajectory approach shots at the mercy of the prevailing ocean winds.

The clubhouse, snugly secure against the elements, has the unusual feature of an indoor winter garden. Its upstairs restaurant gives panoramic views over the holes and coastline. To the south, Póvoa de Varzim revives memories of St Andrews seen from the links which, given the often inclement weather, is highly appropriate.

Ponte de Lima

*Golfe Ponte de Lima, Quinta de Pias, Fornelos, 4990
Ponte de Lima*
TEL: *(258) 743414/5* **FAX:** *(258) 743424*
E-MAIL: *info@golfe-pontedelima.com*
LOCATION: *21 miles/34km north of Braga on N201*
COURSE: *18 holes, 6567yd/6005m, par 71, SSS 71*
TYPE OF COURSE: *A mixture of wooded mountain
and level parkland holes with lakes*
DESIGNERS: *Daniel and David Silva (1995)*
GREEN FEES: *EE*
FACILITIES: *Pro shop, cart, trolley and equipment hire,
tuition, driving range, chipping practice area and putting
green, changing facilities, bar and restaurant in clubhouse*
VISITORS: *Welcome; maximum handicap: men 28,
ladies 36*

PONTE DE LIMA

HOLE	YD	M	PAR	HOLE	YD	M	PAR
1	280	256	4	10	339	310	4
2	131	120	3	11	369	337	4
3	680	622	5	12	483	442	4
4	288	263	4	13	535	489	5
5	458	419	4	14	375	343	4
6	317	290	4	15	176	161	3
7	501	458	5	16	430	393	4
8	214	196	3	17	154	141	3
9	404	369	4	18	433	396	4
OUT	3273	2993	36	IN	3294	3012	35

6567YD • 6005M • PAR 71

Few fledgling golf architects would expect to achieve success from the start, even less so over a difficult site of mixed elevation and severe contours. But at Ponte de Lima, Daniel and David Silva, Portugal's best-known professional players, have had a considerable triumph in their first venture in their homeland. Opened in 1995, this is the most northerly course in the country, set deep in the Costa Verde some 12 miles/20km inland from the sea.

The location, in a wooded mountain area, divides neatly into two quite distinct areas. The first nine holes run up and over a steeply sloped, forested mountainside with chestnut, English and cork oaks while the back nine, in complete contrast, follow comparatively level land through ancient farms of the Quinta de Pias valley, negotiating, as hazards, a series of lakes and winding streams. Here former vineyards, cornfields and fruit orchards form the course.

As an example of golfing design, the brothers Silva have made some extremely daunting challenges highly playable. The holes are very fair, despite the sometimes severe gradients, providing exciting, enjoyable golf. The site is blessed with a wealth of mature trees and offers genuinely spectacular views from the higher ground over the Lima Valley and towards Viana do Castelo. This is most notable at the signature hole – the 8th – where the breathtaking vista may make it difficult to concentrate on matters in hand.

Two of the most striking holes occur in the front nine. The 3rd, whose 680yd/622m double dogleg can fairly claim to be one of the longest in Europe, sounds a monster but is mercifully all downhill. The drive is played down through a chute of tall trees and

Above: A superb par 3 matched by the view, the 8th hole is the ultimate challenge (see page 53).

requires good placement to follow the fairway around to the right while avoiding a long narrow pond to the left. The approach to the small angled green, protected by two bunkers, may require quite a long club or, perhaps more prudently, a lay-up and a pitch.

The other great hole is the par-3 8th, set high on the course and offering extensive views over the surrounding countryside. The hole itself is the stuff of nightmares. Played from an elevated tee, the green beckons temptingly a mere 214yd/196m below. A deep wooded ravine left with out-of-bounds is on the direct line to the pin. The green itself is a slightly elevated plateau amid a sea of troubles and has steep slopes on three sides. There are no bunkers here but what there is is tough enough. Handicap players can aim short right to a patch of fairway among sparse trees.

Another good hole is the 12th, 484yd/443m rated par 4. The tee shot must avoid a pond and creek on the left plus out-of-bounds to the right on a dogleg curving sharply right. Negotiating a stream crossing the fairway and the boundary all the way down the right-hand side, your second shot must hold a green well-protected by a lake eating in from the left. It is deservedly stroke 1 on the card.

SWINGING SOUTH IN NUMBERS

Golf is growing, but not always for the same reasons. In northern Europe, the game is becoming increasingly popular and players, frustrated by winter conditions at home, have turned in numbers to Portugal's sunny fairways. After Britain, with roughly 4 million domestic players, comes Sweden (440,000), Germany (300,000), France (270,000), plus the Netherlands, Denmark, Norway and Finland adding another 310,000. Portugal, on the other hand, only ranks 11th in Continental Europe for total courses and has but 12,000 players. But with Spain, it heads the list for resort locations.

7 🏌 *Vidago*

Golf de Vidago, Pavilhão do Golfe, 5425 Vidago
TEL: *(276) 907356* **FAX:** *(276) 907359*
LOCATION: *9 miles / 15km south-west of Chaves on N2*
COURSE: *9 holes, 2592yd/2370m, par 33, SSS 64*
TYPE OF COURSE: *Short parkland course with well-established trees*
DESIGNER: *Mackenzie Ross (1936)*
GREEN FEES: *EE*
FACILITIES: *Golf shop, trolley hire, caddies, putting green, facilities in nearby Vidago Palace Hotel include bar, restaurant, swimming pool, sauna, tennis*
VISITORS: *Welcome*

Tucked away in the north-east of the country, not far from Chaves (famous for its smoked ham), the well-established nine-hole course at Vidago provides a pleasant contrast to the more frantic, demanding golf of the tourist coasts. Part of the Vidago spa resort, it has charmed holiday golfers for more than half a century with its natural beauty.

Laid out in 1936, it was an early effort by Mackenzie Ross, who was to rebuild Turnberry at the end of World War II. The holes, full of interest and not overlong, are built around a winding stream. Mature pine, oak and cedar trees underline Vidago's place in Portuguese golfing history. It makes a very pleasant spot for a relaxing holiday of which golf is a part rather than a priority.

8 🏌 *Montebelo*

Golf Montebelo, 3510 Farminhão, Viseu
TEL: *(232) 856464* **FAX:** *(276) 856401*
LOCATION: *8 miles / 12km south-west of Viseu off N3*
COURSE: *18 holes, 6908yd/6317m, par 72, SSS 72*
TYPE OF COURSE: *Mountain golf over hilly, forested terrain*
DESIGNERS: *Mark Stilwell and Malcolm Kenyon (1997)*
GREEN FEES: *EE*
FACILITIES: *Pro shop, cart, trolley and equipment hire, tuition, driving range, putting green, changing facilities, bar and restaurant in clubhouse*
VISITORS: *Welcome*

Breaking new ground may historically be a Portuguese trait but in the world of holiday golfing, location demands careful choice. In this fast-expanding field, Montebelo opens up a new destination, being the first course in the northern Beiras region, deep in the heart of dramatic mountain country between the heights of the Serra da Estrela, noted for winter sports, and the Serra do Caramelo with its spa and natural springs.

Near the historic town of Viseu and eminently reachable via the IP3 and IP5 motorways, this new course covers nearly 500 acres/200ha, and makes full use of the undulating terrain, running through valleys lined with pine forest and native flora, over hills, plateaux, some tight doglegs and down steep inclines to fast greens. The clubhouse offers breathtaking views and is part of a hotel, sports and entertainment development in the area, breaking new ground and establishing an attractive inland resort only two hours drive from Lisbon.

Well-established, with many mature trees, the delightfully relaxed setting of the Vidago golf course is part of its charm.

REGIONAL DIRECTORY

Where to Stay

Oporto **Ipanema Park Hotel** (22 610 4174, Fax 22 610 2809) A well-appointed hotel in an excellent position, having fine views of the Douro River and sea plus easy access to both the airport and A1 highway. Five-star service and comfort are evident in the tasteful rooms and elegant restaurant with a respected menu. There is an indoor pool, jacuzzi, sauna, gymnasium, solarium and tennis.

Le Meridien Park Atlantic (22 607 2500, Fax 22 600 2031) is a fine modern 5-star deluxe hotel with all the facilities and refinement to be expected under the Meridien banner. With 232 well-appointed rooms, opportunities for local and international dining, friendly bars, discotheque, spacious snooker room and private underground parking, this is an ideal location, just 15 minutes from the international airport and 10 from the nearest beach.

Porto Palaçio (22 608 6600, Fax 22 609 1467) Well-sited in the heart of the city's new business and shopping area, a short drive from the airport and even less to the host of wine lodges just across the river, this smart modern hotel has 251 rooms and every comfort. Athletic guests, when not golfing, can play squash, tennis, visit the health club with heated pool, jacuzzi, gymnasium, turkish bath, massage and hairdresser.

Espinho **Hotel Solverde Espinho** (22 731 3162, Fax: 22 731 3200). Recently opened and located right by the Praia da Granja beach facing the sea, this hotel has plenty to keep you active. Apart from the nearby golf at Espinho and Miramar, there are both indoor and outdoor heated pools, health club, gym, sauna, jacuzzi, turkish bath, tennis and squash. The restaurant is recommended; also the Solverde Casino close by.

Viana do Castelo **Pousada do Monte Santa Luiza** (258 828 889, Fax 258 828 892). This palatial building, recently converted to a hotel, surmounts the hilltop, with superb views of the city of Viana do Castelo and the Lima River. Classic, spacious rooms and elegant decor are a feature, as is a menu featuring such delights as gratinated hake with mayonnaise, roasted pork loin with paprika and local Viana tart.

Vidago **Vidago Palace Hotel** (276 907 356, Fax 276 907 359) People have been coming to this truly palatial hotel for the spa waters since 1910 (the golf arrived 26 years later). Although fully renovated and modernized, it retains all the grandeur and charm of a bygone age. There are three bars and two dining rooms, one specializing in regional cuisine. Apart from the golf course, there is tennis, cycling, mini-golf, badminton, boating and an outdoor pool, where lunch is served in summer.

Where to Eat

Apart from the city of Oporto, where there is a broad selection of pleasant restaurants not actually in the main hotels, reliable dining is harder to find outside in the surrounding area, but many hotels offer inventive regional menus. In Oporto, try the well-established **Majestic** (22 200 3887) and **Abadia** (22 800 8757), which has a reputation for traditional Portuguese cuisine. In Vila Nova de Gaia, across the river in port wineland, two hotels have recommended restaurants. **Telhados** (22 379 6051), in the Holiday Inn, offers a dramatic riverside view. The other is **Quinta San Salvador** (22 370 2575) in the 4-star *estalagem* of the same name. For something completely different, book a panoramic cruise on the Douro River to see the magnificent terraced vineyards over a full or half-day with bar and tasteful dining on board. Contact Barcadouro (22 200 8882).

What to See

There are plenty of fine buildings and museums in the historic city of **Oporto**, the second largest in the country. Visit the Cathedral with its Romanesque and Baroque features, including a 17th-century chased silver altarpiece. South and west from the cathedral lies the fascinating 'old quarter', leading down to the corbelled houses on the **Quay de Ribeira** along the river's edge. The **Stock Exchange Palace** includes an unusual 19th-century Arab Salon, finely decorated after the style of the Alhambra in Granada. Another church of interest is St Clara's, with an interior entirely lined with 17th-century carved and gilded woodwork.

Find time to sample the port vintages at **Vila Nova da Gaia** (on Oporto's south bank), where the 16 major shippers hold regular tastings. Delicate filigree gold and silver jewellery is made at **Gondomar**, 4 miles/7km away. Not far from Amarante, **Guimarães** has a magnificently well-preserved historic centre and the **Palace of the Dukes of Bragança**, with ceilings of oak and chestnut in its halls, superb tapestries, Persian carpets, Chinese porcelain and a collection of paintings, weapons and armour. For casinos, go to **Espinho** or **Povoa de Varzim.**

Chapter 4

Madeira and Azores

A part of Portuguese maritime history since the 15th century, the island groups of Madeira and the Azores surge up out of the Atlantic, the latter roughly one quarter of the way to America. They were annexed for Portugal by Henry the Navigator and formed convenient ports of call for ships laden with spices from the East or treasure from the Americas, as well as being militarily strategic. Today, they are colourful stops on the itineraries of holiday cruise liners.

Madeira

Fittingly described as the 'jewel of the Atlantic', this dramatic volcanic island thrusts up out of the sea 600 miles/1000km south-west of Lisbon and 500 miles/800km off the coast of Africa. Discovered by Portuguese navigators in 1419, it has served as an important port of call for centuries and its mild climate, ranging between 61°F/16°C and 77°F/25°C, has made it a favoured winter holiday destination.

Left: The town of Angra do Heroismo, on Terceira in the Azores, clusters around a sheltered bay. Above: Grand-stand view of Funchal from the Palheiro clubhouse, Madeira.

Madeira, with its rich volcanic soil and ideal climate, is a floating tropical garden. Despite its severe topography, it grows and exports a profusion of flowers, most notably orchids and strelitzias, or 'bird-of-paradise' flowers. Crops include sugar cane, bananas, passion fruit, avocados, papayas, mangoes and grapes, the latter grown on steeply ascending terraces to create the island's most famous export, Madeira wine.

The sweep of luxury hotels lining the bay of Funchal, the capital, which sprawls back up the hillside, has attracted a well-to-do winter holiday market. There is much to do and see in Funchal as well as up the steep winding roads to the island interior.

Be sure to visit Terreiro da Luta where, as well as getting a fine view down over Funchal, you can take a manned wooden sleigh ride down steep cobbled streets – a unique Madeiran experience. You should also visit the little fishing port of Camara de Lobos, source of the black *espada* (swordfish), caught at depths of up to 10,000ft/3,000m. Inland, beyond plunging valleys, spectacular waterfalls and

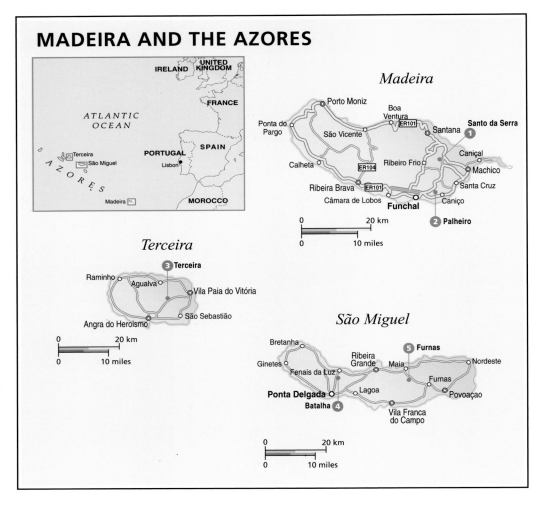

MADEIRA AND THE AZORES

dense untamed vegetation, is the remote village of Curral das Freiras in the crater of an extinct volcano, where nuns hid from pillaging pirates in the 16th century.

As souvenirs, you can buy fine embroidery and tapestry work, as well as a wide range of wicker products, from small baskets to suites of furniture. Leatherwork is another speciality. Gourmets will appreciate the selection of fresh fish and seafood, which, in addition to the aforementioned swordfish, includes tuna, red mullet, sea bream and mackerel. Look also for *espetadas* (meat cooked on a laurel spit) and honey cakes. Finally, try the

famed Madeira wine, fortified and produced by a method that replicates the conditions experienced during the long voyage by sail to England in the 18th century. It comes in varying degrees of sweetness: Malmsey (the sweetest), Bual, Verdelho and Sercial.

Azores

Only two of the nine islands of the Azores, San Miguel and Terceira, currently have golf. They offer rugged coastlines with sheer cliffs leading to inland plateaux and green, fertile valleys. Dormant volcanos provide crystal lakes, thermal

springs and boiling mud, the latter used to cook *cozido* (meat and vegetables) by volcanic heat. The islands benefit from unpolluted air and a mild climate, tempered by the Gulf Stream, where the temperature ranges between 57°F/14°C and 72°F/22°C. However, you can experience all the seasons in a day, with sunshine one minute and thick cloud descending the volcanic slopes the next.

There is much to admire in the main towns, where the architecture, mostly dating from the 17th and 18th centuries, contrasts white façades with black local basalt. Both Ponta Delgada on San Miguel, and Angra do Heroismo on Terceira – the latter nominated by UNESCO as a World Heritage site – reflect their long history in churches, forts and museums. The fertile countryside is full of flowers, especially *hortensia* (hydrangeas), as well as hibiscus, rhododendrons and azaleas, and produces pineapples, tea, tobacco, dairy products,

Camara de Lobos, a quaint Madeira fishing village just along the coast from Funchal, was a favourite painting location for Sir Winston Churchill.

mahogany and cedar wood.

Longstanding folk traditions are preserved in numerous colourful festivals and processions. One unusual pastime is 'bullfighting' in the streets, with the animal restrained by a rope. Shoppers should look for weaving, embroidery, lace and basketwork or the products of local ingenuity made from fig tree pith, fish scales or wheat straw. Diners can enjoy a broad harvest of fresh fish and shellfish, including lobster, crab, octopus stewed in wine, goose barnacles and limpets with rice. Meat dishes include pork sausage, served with yam. There are local cows' and goats' milk cheeses and an interesting choice of traditional desserts and pastries, to be washed down with the local Biscoitos wine or pineapple and passion fruit liqueurs.

1 Santo da Serra

Clube de Golf Santo da Serra, Sto António da Serra, 9200 Machico, Madeira
TEL: *(291) 552345* **FAX:** *(091) 552367*
E-MAIL: *golf.santoserra@mail.telepac.pt*
LOCATION: *6 miles/10km west of Machico on N675 to Sto da Serra*
COURSES: *18 holes (Machico and Desertas), 6636yd/6068m, par 72, SSS 72; also 9 holes (Serras), 3204yd/2930m, par 36*
TYPE OF COURSE: *Plateau parkland at altitude with many mature trees, some slopes and deep ravines*
DESIGNER: *Robert Trent Jones (1991)*
GREEN FEES: *EEE*
FACILITIES: *Pro shop, cart, trolley and equipment hire, caddies, tuition, driving range, putting green, changing facilities, snack bar, restaurant*
VISITORS: *Welcome*

HOLE	YD	M	PAR	HOLE	YD	M	PAR
1	406	371	4	10	353	323	4
2	410	375	4	11	569	520	5
3	520	476	5	12	315	288	4
4	220	201	3	13	459	420	4
5	419	383	4	14	348	318	4
6	348	318	4	15	189	173	3
7	532	487	5	16	492	450	5
8	149	136	3	17	172	157	3
9	349	319	4	18	386	353	4
OUT	3353	3066	36	IN	3283	3002	36

SANTO DA SERRA

6636YD · 6068M · PAR 72

There are, not surprisingly, strong historic connections between golf and alcohol. In the case of Portuguese golf, two of its earliest courses owe their origins to the influence of British wine producers. Following the example of the port shippers in Oporto, it was natural that another British contingent, those involved with the wines of Madeira, should create their own course. The only semi-level land available on this sheer volcanic outcrop was high up on the plateau slopes of the island at Santo da Serra, and a fairly rustic nine-hole course was opened in 1936. The following year, a group of five top British professionals of the day – J. H. Taylor, Alf Padgham, Abe Mitchell, Bill Cox and Allan Dailey – were invited out on the liner *Arundel Castle* to play an exhibition.

The nine-hole course remained for more than 50 years, little changed and often lost in low cloud, until Robert Trent Jones was invited to conceive a 27-hole layout on the same site. The first 18 holes – the Machico and Desertas nines – were opened in 1991, while the third loop, Serras, came into play recently.

Golf at Santo da Serra is, in many respects, 'golf in heaven', set at 2,100ft/640m above sea level. There are amazing views down to verdant valleys, distant coastal villages, offshore islands and, occasionally, golf seemingly floating in space above the cloud layer. Despite its mountainous situation, there are relatively few steeply sloping holes. The designer has skilfully created a course which follows plateaux and ledges to well-shaped greens, often with career carries over cavernous ravines where any ball is irretrievable. The setting is lush, floral and essentially fair; there are always safer options for the less confident

but, whatever level of golf you play, the views are glorious.

The PGA European Tour has visited the course for the Madeira Open since 1993 and the competitors have been impressed, both with the condition of the course and its spectacular setting. With mature trees and a wealth of wild flora, golfing here is equally a journey through a tropical garden. There are many outstanding holes where changes of elevation and altitude will affect club selection. Undoubtedly two of the finest come early in the Machico nine.

The 3rd hole is a double-dogleg 520yd/476m par 5, played from a funnel of trees onto a narrow plateau. This curves tightly round a cavernous abyss to the left, thick with natural vegetation and falling to the valley far below. Caution is the key, since the slope is to the left and a hook is to perdition. The plateau green sits above the fairway, a green shelf falling away left and rear, seemingly suspended in space. It is dramatic

The approach shot on the 520yd/476m double-dogleg par-5 3rd, to a plateau green framed by mountains. Staying right is paramount, despite the sand. Anything left is a lost ball – don't even bother to look.

stuff and a par is well-earned, since the views are highly distracting.

Survive the 3rd and the spectacular 4th awaits. This is a par 3 at the end of the world, 220yd/201m straight across a yawning chasm to a green perched on a summit, with nothing to the left but the view down to the beach and the Atlantic (see page 53).

Another good hole is the 11th, 569yd/520m par 5, played from an elevated tee to a double-dogleg fairway which skirts a mountain lake left and a strategic bunker complex. It is one of the few fairly level holes on the course. Nearing the end, the short 17th can pose problems. Played across a hillside slope from shelf to shelf, with dense bush on both sides, the shot must be well-judged to avoid kicking unplayably left.

 *Palheiro*

*Palheiro Golf, Sitio do Balançal, São Gonçalo, 9000
Funchal, Madeira*
TEL: *(291) 792116* **FAX:** *(291) 792456*
E-MAIL: *jonathan.f@mail.telepac.pt*
LOCATION: *10 miles/16km north-east of Funchal, off
R102 to Camacha*
COURSE: *18 holes, 6588yd/6022m, par 71, SSS 71*
TYPE OF COURSE: *Parkland with many mature trees
located on steeply sloping volcanic site*
DESIGNER: *Cabell Robinson (1994)*
GREEN FEES: *EEE*
FACILITIES: *Pro shop, cart, trolley and equipment hire,
tuition, driving range, putting green, changing facilities, bar
and recommended restaurant in clubhouse*
VISITORS: *Welcome*

B lessed with a sub-tropical climate and, as a
volcanic island, sufficient rainfall, Madeira
is famous for its lush vegetation and produce
such as sugar, bananas and wine. More recently,
the installation of a second golf course in 1994,
near the fabled gardens of Quinta do Palheiro,
has made it an even greater priority with
holiday golfers.

Creating a golf course only 15 minutes'
drive from the capital, Funchal, amongst steep
volcanic slopes and mature vegetation, called
for no little skill and experience. Cabell
Robinson, who formerly worked with Robert
Trent Jones, has proved worthy of the task.
Apart from the 1st, 3rd and 4th holes, which
run up and down a very severe hillside indeed,
the architect has found many attractive
situations. Close by the ancient Palheiro estate,
with its wealth of specimen trees brought from
around the world, the holes are both fair and
playable, with many also affording quite
sensational views out over the town of Funchal
way below, the sea and the distant islands.

Lush Bermuda fairways and subtle, speedy
greens put your game to the test; that is, if you
can take your eyes off the panoramic views.
The clubhouse, attractively built in local style,
has a patio view over the whole of Funchal
spread out below: supported by a glass of
Madeira wine, an unforgettable experience.

*An approach shot view of the 3rd, a steeply downhill par
4 of 405yd/370m to a receptive green over water. The
clubhouse beyond has a spectacular terrace view.*

3 Terceira

*Clube de Golfe da Ilha Terceira, Caixa Postal 15, 9760
Praia da Vitória, Terceira, Azores*
TEL: *(295) 92444* **FAX:** *(295) 92445*
LOCATION: *North-east of Angra do Heroísmo on road to
Vila Nova*
COURSE: *18 holes, 6227yd/5655m, par 72, SSS 70*
TYPE OF COURSE: *Gently undulating parkland with
mature trees*
DESIGNER: *Unknown (1954)*
GREEN FEES: *EE*
FACILITIES: *Pro shop, cart, trolley and equipment hire,
caddies, tuition, driving range, putting green, tennis,
changing facilities, bar and restaurant in clubhouse*
VISITORS: *Always welcome*

*Putting on the steeply sloped 18th green, a fine finishing
hole despite being par 3, and easy on the eye, with ranks
of hydrangeas bordering the clubhouse, along with flower
beds, pampas grass and cedar trees.*

There is a distinctly transatlantic flavour here, which is hardly surprising since the club had its origins in nine holes built by US Air Force personnel in 1952 for their exclusive use. It expanded to 18 holes and open membership in 1954 and today boasts an extensive clubhouse, a mature and interesting 18-hole course and over 1,000 members. It offers a very playable, if somewhat prosaic, course designed by enthusiastic amateurs.

The abiding memory is of an extremely well-maintained golf course, where broad fairways are lined with orderly ranks of long-established evergreen Japanese cedars. Laid out more than 1,200ft/350m above sea level, it is also blessed with a profusion of colourful flowers, most notably hydrangeas of varying hues, to the point where the experience is more akin to playing in a tropical garden.

With wide, sometimes sloping fairways and elevated, holding greens, this is a course for golfers of all levels. Superbly kept, especially the fast greens, it has many holes of considerable charm plus a notable finish. The 17th, 501yd/461m par 5, demands consideration of a transverse fairway ditch affecting the second shot and a lake immediately fronting a tilted green. The best, however, is saved to last. The 18th is a mere 137yd/125m but has an acknowledged

reputation. All uphill from the tee, players have to clear a water hazard and sand as well as avoiding a large tree encroaching from the left. The green is severely sloped back towards the tee and is treacherous. Hole out and the friendly bar of this very social members' club is close by. It is a beautifully maintained and pleasantly unpretentious club, where visitors are made very welcome.

AZULEJOS
AS YOU LIKE THEM

There is nothing more typically Portuguese, appearing on walls, street signs, and any number of other outdoor and indoor locations, than the blue and white hand-painted tiles called azulejos. Derived from the Arabic *al zuleiq*, meaning small polished stone, they have become an essential part of architectural decoration since first becoming popular during the 16th century. They trace a continuing link in the nation's artistic heritage, decorated with birds, flowers, people and abstract designs. Even complete pictures showing Biblical or historical scenes, made up of mosaics of individual tiles, have survived through the ages.

 ## Batalha

Batalha Golf Course,'Verde Golf Country Club,
Rua do Bom Jesus, Aflitos, 9545 Fenais da Luz,
São Miguel, Azores
TEL: *(296) 498540* **FAX:** *(296) 498284*
LOCATION: *15 minutes from Ponta Delgada on road north
to Fenais da Luz*
COURSE: *18 holes, 7037yd/6435m, par 72, SSS 73*
TYPE OF COURSE: *Sloping mountain golf with mature trees*
DESIGNERS: *Cameron Powell Associates (1996)*
GREEN FEES: *EE*
FACILITIES: *Pro shop, cart, trolley and equipment hire,
tuition, driving range, chipping practice area, two large
putting greens, bar and two restaurants in clubhouse*
VISITORS: *Handicap certificate required; maximum: men
28, ladies 36; dress code; soft spikes only*

This new course, named after the site of a former battle between the Spanish and Portuguese just a short distance from Ponta Delgada, has the same owner and management as its sister further east on the island, yet the two are as different as chalk and cheese. Created by the designers of the newer holes at Furnas, Batalha has been planned to a championship specification and built with a broad brush over rolling land and the lower mountain slopes of the area. The course is eventually to have 27 holes, and has Bermuda fairways and Pennlinks greens. Although some holes wind past tall trees (mostly eucalyptus)

*The ocean view behind the par-3 15th is just another
distraction on a dramatic 213yd/195m downhill hole,
well defended by trees and encircling sand.*

and areas of dense natural vegetation, many flow over relatively open land, where steep slopes, lakes, old stone walls, sand and sea breezes provide a serious test.

Many of the holes require careful club judgement, being steeply up- or downhill to deep, elevated greens, where a 55yd/50m putt is quite possible. The putting surfaces are fair, with relatively little movement and, from the higher holes, offer spectacular views along the coastline or out to sea. Three holes encapsulate the challenge of Batalha. The 4th, a par 5 of 611yd/559m, is a lengthy uphill dogleg left which offers a long carry over water to cut the corner. The 6th, 459yd/420m, plunges downhill across a deep fairway valley and up to a blind elevated green. The signature hole is the par-3 15th, blessed with fine ocean views from the tee well above the green, which sits 213yd/195m below.

The large modern, well-equipped clubhouse has fine views from the upper floor restaurants. Batalha has great potential which should be fulfilled as it matures.

Furnas

Furnas Golf Course, Verde Golf Country Club, Achada das Furnas, 9675 Furnas, San Miguel, Azores
TEL: *(296) 498559* **FAX:** *(296) 498284*
LOCATION: *40 minutes from Ponta Delgada, taking road through Furnas and Pedras do Galego*
COURSE: *18 holes, 6815yd/6232m, par 72, SSS 72*
TYPE OF COURSE: *Mature undulating parkland with lakes and well-established tall evergreens*
DESIGNERS: *Mackenzie Ross (9 holes); Cameron Powell Associates (9 holes) (1939/1990)*
GREEN FEES: *EE*
FACILITIES: *Pro shop, cart, trolley and equipment hire, caddies, tuition, two putting greens, practice tee and chipping area, changing facilities, bar and restaurant in clubhouse*
VISITORS: *Welcome; maximum handicap: men 28, ladies 36*

Located in an area of outstanding natural beauty, close to the Furnas lake and its thermal springs, the course is a happy marriage of old and new laid out against a gentle backdrop of wooded hills. The original nine holes were created in 1939 by the Scottish architect Mackenzie Ross, also noted for his work at Estoril and Vidago (see pages 76 and 98) and for his restoration of Turnberry after World War II. These nine holes rank among the earliest created in Portugal and sit closest to the clubhouse, flanked by towering Japanese cedars and clumps of colourful hydrangeas, azaleas and tall pampas grass. The later holes

(the course was extended to 18 by British designers Cameron Powell in 1990) have been seamlessly added in the spirit and style of the original. In place of the majestic evergreens, palms and other attractive varieties have been planted along with the addition of four new water hazards.

Despite the course's location – at the heart of a volcanic island in a mid-Atlantic region noted for its mild and unpolluted environment – Ross was able to build in many design features common to some of the great Scottish courses. These, when combined with the now towering cedar trees, present a genuine examination. The conditions are lush and holding, which is just as well since many greens are small, elevated and with fiendish contours. The newer holes continue the theme, substituting penal water in some cases for the lack of trees, though the surrounding forested volcanic outcrops play their part.

The low-level clubhouse has an astonishing 240° panoramic view over much of the course and is under the management of Verde Golf Country Club, along with Batalha.

Japanese cedars contrast with more open holes, where bunkers, small greens and startegic water govern play.

REGIONAL DIRECTORY

MADEIRA
Where to Stay
Funchal **The Cliff Bay Resort Hotel** (291 707 0707, Fax 291 76 2524). Occupying a spectacular cliff-top garden setting on Funchal Bay, this luxurious hotel has excellent facilities including three restaurants, two pools, spa bath, sauna, steam room, tennis, squash, many watersports and a complimentary shuttle with reduced fees at Palheiro Golf. **Reid's Palace** (291 71 7171, Fax 291 71 7177) is part of Madeira's history and the hotel by which others are judged. Stylish comfort and discreet service with facilities to match. A selection of restaurants, two heated pools, tennis. table tennis, snooker, sauna, massage, sailing and other watersports. **Madeira Palacio** (291 76 4476, Fax 291 76 4477). Recently renovated, this elegant hotel is surrounded by tropical gardens in a spectacular setting above the sea. Three restaurants, bars, large heated pool, sauna, massage and a selection of shops. Special terms for golfers.
Machico **Dom Pedro Baia** (291 965 751, Fax 291 966 889). Located at Machico, an undisturbed bay just past the airport and handy for the golf at Santo da Serra, this 4-star hotel offers friendly service and a good choice of facilities including indoor and outdoor pools, tennis, squash, scuba dive instruction and a range of shops.

Where to Eat
There are a few restaurants in downtown Funchal, a short stroll from the vast curve of hotels around the bay, but the plethora of good hotel restaurants ensures an excellent selection of gourmet dining to suit all tastes, many with spectacular panoramic views of the sea. **Casa Velha** (291 725 676) has an outdoor cocktail terrace and an international menu. **Golfinho** (291 726 774) specializes in seafood as does **Estrela do Mar** (291 728 255).

What to See
Madeira is a floating garden, a verdant green volcanic outcrop where many varieties of tropical flowers grow in profusion. Visit the **Botanical Gardens** in Funchal; also the **Jardim Municipal** and **Parque da Cidade**. The oldest church is the 15th-century **Funchal Cathedral Se**, which has a Manueline pulpit and a cedarwood ceiling inlaid with ivory. Go to the **Mercado dos Lavradores** (Farmers' Market) for all the colour and bustle of the real thing. **Cabo Girão**, west of Funchal, is the second highest cliff in the world. Inland, **Pico Ruivo** (6,109ft/1,862m) marks the highest point on the island with fine views. Also visit the deep extinct crater village of **Curral das Freiras.**

AZORES
Where to Stay
Terceira **Albergeria Cruzeiro** (295 217 071, Fax 295 217 075). In the centre of Angra, facing a charming leafy square, there is a warm welcome at this 4-star inn. The 3-star **Angra Hotel** (295 217 041, Fax: 295 217 049), in the main square of Angra do Heroísmo, has two restaurants, bar, solarium and is fully air-conditioned.
San Miguel **Hotel Atlantico** (296 302 200, Fax 296 302 209). On the Ponta Delgada harbour front, this 4-star hotel has 140 rooms; all have a balcony sea view. **Senhora da Rosa** (296 628 150, Fax 296 629 939). This 4-star low-rise *estalagem* is set on a quiet estate near Ponta Delgada. It has only 28 rooms, each beautifully decorated, and a pleasant bar and restaurant.

Where to Eat
Terceira In Agra, **O Pescador** (295 513 495) specializes in seafood rice and *cataplanas* of fish and shellfish. **Marcelino's Bar** (295 215 828) is noted for steaks and *acatra* regional. **Restaurant Zenite** (212 260) has a reputation for oven-baked salt cod and traditional Portuguese stews, including fish. At Porto S, Mateus, visit the popular **Restorante Beira Mar** (642 392) for fresh fish and shellfish with a view.
San Miguel In Ponta Delgada, specialities at **Casa Marisco** (296 382 780) include grilled limpets and baked octopus. **O Robonto** (296 283 769) offers an international menu, fresh shellfish and a sea view. **Barracuda** (296 381 421) has fresh fish and shellfish plus an attractive view of the ocean. **Cantinho do Cou** (296 287 052) offers many regional dishes. For steaks, go to **Restaurant Alcides** (296 282 677). Near Furnas, **O Miroma** (296 584 422) and **Restaurante Tony's** (296 584 290) both cook dishes in the hot springs.

What to See
Terceira Visit the **Cathedral**, the 16th-century **Castle of São João Baptista**, the Baroque-styled **Bettencourt Palace** and the **Museum of Angra do Heroísmo** in the old Convent of São Francisco and its adjacent church. The **Alta da Memoria** gives a superb view of the town and Monte Brasil. There is an interesting wine museum at **Biscoitos**.
San Miguel See the great 7.5 mile/12km crater at **Sete Cidades**. Near the golf at **Furnas** are natural hot springs; there is also the tranquil beauty of the **Furnas Lake**. Pineapple production is on show at Faja de Baixo and, in town, the **Carlos Machado Museum** in the old Monastery of Santo André has an interesting natural history and marine collection as well as paintings, sculptue and jewellery.